A BLOODY SUMMER

to Amelie

A BLOODY SUMMER

THE IRISH AT THE BATTLE OF BRITAIN

Dan Harvey

MERRION
PRESS

First published in 2020 by
Merrion Press
10 George's Street
Newbridge
Co. Kildare
Ireland
www.merrionpress.ie

9781785373251 (Paper)
9781785373268 (Kindle)
9781785373275 (Epub)

A CIP catalogue record for this book is
available from the British Library.

Front cover: Battle of Britain. Czech Hurricane pilots in 1940 at their
squadron's UK base © Pictorial Press Ltd / Alamy Stock Photo.

Back cover: RAF Hawker Hurricanes making a head-on attack against
German Luftwaffe Messerschmitt Bf 110s in the Battle of Britain
© Gary Eason / Flight Artworks / Alamy Stock Photo.

Merrion Press is a member of Publishing Ireland.

CONTENTS

FOREWORD

Growing up, one of the first movies that my father brought me to see was *633 Squadron* – an action air picture based on events during the Second World War and featuring the ubiquitous DH Mosquito aircraft, the 'Wooden Wonder'. This outstanding picture and iconic aircraft caught my attention and I commenced building AirFix models as fast as they and I could make them. Along the way I assembled a sample of the Supermarine Spitfire, featuring in another film *Angels 15*, as well as *Reach for the Sky* and many more. Around the end of the Sixties the film *Battle of Britain* was released and I splashed out on a massive 1/48th scale model to celebrate. My mother asked me what I was building and I said I'd give her a hint, saying 'RJ Mitchell'. 'Oh,' she replied, 'a Spitfire!' I was stunned – and impressed! But I learnt then that my parents had lived through the war and blitz in Belfast and were well aware of the origins and importance of Mitchell's creation.

They moved to Dublin after the war and I grew up in a community in Malahide comprising an amazing amount of former Second World War ex-RAF pilots flying with Aer Lingus. Jock Smith had flown Consolidated Liberator bombers in the Far East theatre of operations and Roy Smith flew Lancaster bombers on missions over Europe and had a wonderful photograph on the wall in his hallway of his squadron personnel posing in front of a Lancaster bomber.

Ian Dunlop was a fighter pilot who flew in the Battle of Britain and met his future wife between scrambles during the battle as she was a WAAF technician and involved in servicing on his aircraft! After the battle, he served in the Aircraft and Armament Experimental Establishment at Boscombe Down where he test-flew every Allied fighter type including P-51s, P-47s, and P-38s, as well as the RAF types like Typhoons and all the Spitfire marks, assessing them for combat performance and handling qualities.

During my service in the Air Corps I became aware that they had operated a squadron of Supermarine Seafire LF. IIIs Mk.47s and then replaced them in the early Fifties with six, two-seat conversion, Spitfire T.Mk.9s. Long since gone before my entry to the Flying School there were reports that they had been sold to the Battle of Britain film company and that some were still airworthy in the UK in private hands. In 1986 one returned to Casement Aerodrome in the ownership of Mr Nick Grace to display at that year's Air Spectacular airshow. Sadly, Nick later died in a car crash but the aircraft has returned since to our skies, displayed by his wife Carolyn and son Richard. The sound of that Rolls Royce Merlin engine combined with its speed and the elegance of its wings made a big impression on me as a lowly Marchetti pilot!

Twenty years on and another ex-Air Corps Spitfire, formerly serial number '161', graced our skies once again to attend a 'Wings Day', sponsored this time by the airline CityJet. It was and remains in the ownership of John Romain of the Historic Aircraft Restoration Company based in the former RAF base Duxford and its appearance and aerobatic display at the end of the parade was both inspirational and impressive. After landing it formed a stunning backdrop for the photographs of the graduating class, dominating the apron with its mighty propeller while the engine clicked and ticked as it cooled off.

A couple of weeks later I was fortunate to fly in her back to Duxford, helping John navigate through and out of Irish Airspace and being allowed to hand fly her all the way to our destination where he then put on a spirited aerobatics display before landing. I sat in the back, a passenger, and experienced the sheer power and manoeuvrability of that aircraft and was enthralled by its noise and performance. I have heard the cockpit noise of a Spitfire likened to driving around inside the China Showrooms at full power in a JCB and I must admit it comes close to fitting the bill. On parking we were met by the aircraft's technical team, who gave her a thorough and loving examination, confessing as they did, that they had missed her in their hangar. Such is the magic and magnetism of a Spitfire.

I flew an ex-Air Corps Spitfire once more in my career – Nick Grace's machine, piloted by his son Richard. Strapped into that small but comfortable cockpit, it's an aircraft that you 'wear' when the straps are tightened. He gave me control to get a feel for her and the response took me by surprise. We both 'blacked out' on my first attempt at a loop! In fairness, Richard did warn me about that element of Spitfire control sensitivity before we took-off and from then on I explored with a little more caution the full flight spectrum and enjoyed about fifteen minutes of basic aerobatics over County Kildare in his company.

The seventieth anniversary of the Battle of Britain came around in 2010 and into the Office of the GOC Air Corps arrived an invitation from the Chief of the Air Staff of the RAF to attend the laying up of the Fighter Command 'colours' in Westminster Cathedral. Times had moved on; the veterans were not getting any younger and parading to the cathedral was becoming impossible for many of them as they approached their nineties. This event was to mark the end of their 'Battle' parades and my presence was to represent the many Irishmen from the Republic who had fought in the Battle – thirteen in all, I was informed. Allocated a seat in the Poets' Corner, along with a large cohort of military attachés and European Air Chiefs, I watched as the veterans were arranged opposite us, some in wheelchairs. There before me were the surviving pilots, technicians, armourers, radar operators, sector fighter controllers and group headquarters staffs who had actually fought the battle. These were the very people who wouldn't give up, ever, never, no matter what the odds in 1940, when all of Europe had been suborned by the mighty and apparently invincible military forces of the Third Reich. Medals adorned every chest and they carried themselves with an air of defiance, or stubbornness, or arrogance, or perhaps all three.

The Fighter Command colours were carried into the cathedral by Geoffrey Wellum, author of the classic Battle of Britain fighter pilot's memoir *First Light* and one of the youngest pilots involved in the Battle. Now he was one of The Few capable of carrying the weight of their colours and he proudly led the parade past assembled serving and former prime ministers, senior military officers and guests, to hand them over to Prince Charles, parading that day in his RAF uniform. It was an honour to be invited to attend and experience such a moving finale to the Battle and see at first hand those who had 'been there, done that'.

The Battle of Britain Day celebrations are still a significant annual event in the RAF to this day, with active bases celebrating on 15 September. Initially my access to such events was facilitated by the Station Commander in RAF Aldergrove, a station which enjoyed a long and cordial friendship with the Air Corps. It was always instructive to see the importance of remembering the Battle emphasised by higher authorities in the RAF and by today's fliers. Even more impressive was the final flypast and victory roll overhead the Officers' Mess by a Spitfire from the Battle of Britain Memorial Flight, at or just before sunset. This pattern is repeated at every airbase and seeing it later at RAF Northolt was also a great privilege, as that base is the last surviving operational air base from the Battle. The place positively reeks of history and this is underlined further by a visit to the Sector Operations Room, lovingly and voluntarily restored by an amateur group of history-minded enthusiasts.

At one such parade I was fortunate to meet with former Flt Lt William Buchanan Walker, who in 2012 was one of the last of The Few to whom so much was owed by The Many. He was shot down over the English Channel. Wounded in the leg and bleeding badly, he baled-out of his stricken Spitfire over the Goodwin Sands. He survived long enough clinging to a wreck on the Sands to be picked up by an RAF rescue launch, only surviving because the cold of the English Channel water stemmed the flow of blood from his wound. During our brief meeting he produced his keyring on which the offending bullet was dangling, extracted by the surgeons during the subsequent surgery on his leg.

William later wrote a poem in tribute to his comrades which is included on the Battle of Britain Memorial on the Cliffs of Dover at Capel-le-Ferne – a stone inscription which lists 2,937 names, some of them Irish, as Dan's book now tells us. William's poem 'Our Wall' tells of the:

> many brave unwritten tales
> That were simply told in vapour trails.

So it can be seen that, for this Irishman, the echoes of the Battle of Britain remain numerous and strong, even so long after the last combat concluded late in 1940. Long hidden shadows cast by

Ireland and Irishmen in RAF service are no longer 'unwritten' and Dan Harvey now exposes their stories, told in detail and sensitively with the Irish context and perspective firmly in focus. Few, if any, books have examined the Battle of Britain from this side of the Irish Sea facing east when then, as now, the fate of our two island nations were never more closely intertwined. What hurts one, hurts all, and the implications for Ireland should England have fallen to the Nazi threat were clearly obvious and are explored in detail by Dan. Irishmen were to play their part in the worldwide conflict in every theatre and every service of every allied nation. It is appropriate that the feats of the Irish airmen who took part in what is probably the most famous air battle in history be recorded and their stories explored and put into context and committed to history.

If you have a love of flight, air battle and history, if you've ever looked up at the sleek shape of a Spitfire in flight and heard its beautiful engine at high power, if you want another window through which to view the Second World War, and the Battle of Britain in particular, then I highly recommend that you read on.

Paul Fry,
Brigadier General (Retd),
General Officer Commanding the Air Corps,
Dublin, Ireland.

PREFACE

The enemy Junkers 88s arrived in their standard V-shaped formation; their Messerschmitt fighter escort, 4,000 feet above and astern them, was ideally placed between the bombers and the sun. The formation's height, bearing and numbers had, however, already been accurately detected and tracked by coastal radar stations. Their intended target anticipated, this was relayed from Fighter Command's fighter control system, through Group Headquarters, to Sector Control, then on to the nearest appropriate airfields – those whose resident squadrons immediately 'scrambled' to intercept the incoming bombers. Scrambled, the Hurricane and Spitfire interceptors were up in the air in minutes, seeking to impede and obstruct; to take the fight to the heart of the enemy attack.

Radar and the Royal Air Force's (RAF) Fighter Command and Control system gave the defenders a distinct advantage, providing an almost 'real time' picture of what was happening in the skies so the British fighters could be in the right place at the right time. This, in 1940, was new and sophisticated. Thereafter, it was height and speed that was important. The other crucial element for success in aerial combat was surprise: a sudden, unexpected attack by British fighters, preferably in numbers, to catch and cut off the main body of enemy bombers.

From early dawn, a large force from the Luftwaffe had launched a continuous series of determined day-time raids on southern English ports and the coastline. The RAF, Irishmen among them, had been involved in several intense aerial engagements, and now, once again, well into the afternoon, they were called into action.

On sighting the Junkers 88s, the Hurricanes, dived into the tight German bomber formation. The bombers broke formation and split in every direction, diving and jinking, some making for the nearest clouds, while their fighter escort entered combat in their defence.

The Spitfires now entered the fray, engaged the Messerschmitts, and a series of ferocious fighter-to-fighter dogfights erupted. The reality of aerial combat, with the high speeds of the fighter aircraft involved, meant that the majority of actual engagements lasted only seconds. It was important to get in close, fire in short bursts, then disengage, using speed to escape the scene. The enemy fighters had descended from above, having peeled off in ones and twos, and opened fire; they dived continuously, climbing up to regain position for a similar manoeuvre.

The RAF Spitfire pilots addressed the Messerschmitt threat while the Hurricane pilots concentrated on the destruction of the German bombers. The main objective was to knock them out of the skies.

One of these RAF pilots, newly qualified with less than ten hours flying time on Spitfires, found himself separated from his squadron leader. Acknowledging his lack of experience, the squadron leader had instructed the 'novice' to stay close; only in the midst of the heightened moment, he had not. Now alone, albeit in a crowded sky, the pilot wondered at the intensity and lightning speed of exchanges, and the manoeuvrings of the individual aircraft. Instinctive reaction was required, and to his horror he realised that he was way off tempo, completely out of sync and hopelessly out of his depth. Discouraged, mixed up, confused, too much was happening too fast; everything was too quick to take in, and by the time he had regained focus, what he was confronted with had changed, and then changed again.

He could not mentally process what was constantly changing in front of him. It was even difficult to tell friend from foe. His inexperience was likely, at any moment, to see him killed, and he was suddenly all too aware of this probability. Then, shockingly, he became conscious of an enemy fighter lining up to make a head-on attack at him, opening fire with his cannons at long range to knock him out of the sky. Wide of the mark with his opening salvo, the enemy fighter gave up his line of attack and broke off overhead. Alarmed and relieved all at once, the pilot's respite was fleeting; in the next instant, he heard the sound of firing. From somewhere in his mind, he remembered his flight instructor once telling him that if he ever found himself in this situation, he was to turn the aircraft immediately – the sound almost certainly came from an enemy fighter attacking from astern. He had the wit to turn sharply and slightly downwards in the recommended evasive manoeuvre; the Spitfire had markedly responsive handling, and it was this instantaneous response that kept him alive as the Messerschmitt cannon shells tore past him. Nonetheless, the Messerschmitt followed, the experienced pilot applying patience in overcoming his aircraft's marginally slower sharp turn to the right. Once executed, the Messerschmitt was on him again.

'Do not fly straight,' an inner voice screamed.

Resisting level flight now became his uppermost thought and he half rolled his Spitfire to the right. The mismatch in experience and skill was not long in telling, and try as he might, the youngster could neither outfly nor outmanoeuvre his pursuer; it seemed that nothing he tried could shake him. He decided his only hope was to outrun him, and even this was not proving successful. His anxiety mounted as his options more or less exhausted themselves. Strain had given way to angst, fretfulness to fear. Almost overwhelmed, he was consumed by an overpowering dread that these were his last moments. This dread reached its extreme when he again heard the sound of firing; he felt certain of the disintegration of his aircraft and him along with it. Instead it was the Messerschmitt that began emitting a trail of dark smoke, and then flames began bellowing from its engine. His squadron leader had picked up on what was happening and positioned himself to the rear of the pursuing Messerschmitt – he got in close behind him, kept his Spitfire's nose on the enemy, and approached its blind spot; when the golden opportunity presented itself – a two to three second window – he fired all eight of his .303" machine guns, recording a further 'kill'. The youngster was spared to live and fight another day. Thoroughly shaken but all the wiser for the experience, he all too readily realised that the day's sortie nearly had a tragic end.

AUTHOR'S NOTE

Flight Officer William Moore, an Irishman, married Cecilia Beck at St Peter's Church, Over Wallop, Hampshire on 4 July 1940. Moore was a pilot of 236 Squadron and operated Blenheims throughout the Battle of Britain.

Among serving pilots and airmen, and later historians, the start and end date of the battle is disputed. Officially, it was from 10 July to 31 October 1940. There were 2,938 British, Allied and other airmen awarded the Battle of Britain clasp for having flown at least one sortie with an accredited unit of RAF Fighter Command during this time. The twin-engine Bristol Blenheim Mk IF aircraft, even then obsolete, were used as fighters by the RAF. These carried an observer and gunner in addition to the pilot – hence the term 'airman' is sometimes used as a catchall denomination. This is certainly the case for those named on the Battle of Britain Monument at Victoria Embankment, London, unveiled in 2005. Interestingly, William Storey Moore is not listed among the names of those coming from Ireland; instead he is found with those listed as coming from Australia. When the names of all Battle of Britain airmen were being drawn up for inclusion on the monument in 2004 and 2005, it was believed that he was an Australian from Melbourne.

However, in late 2012 Australian author and historian Kristen Alexander provided information that William Moore was born in Dublin on 21 November 1916, and educated there until 1932, whereupon he moved to Australia, continuing his schooling there until 1936. His father, William Moore, was from Dundrum, and his mother was from Dartry Road. However, he, 'William Junior', moved to England and joined the RAF on a short service commission in June 1937. During the Battle of Britain, 554 RAF airmen lost their lives; a further 795 were to die before the end of the war. William Moore was among the latter. He was killed on 24 December 1943 acting as squadron leader with 143 Squadron. His Beaufighter XI JM160 (the replacement for the Blenheim) broke up in the air – the cause unknown – while attacking a German Heinkel He 177 bomber over the Bay of Biscay. His widow, Cecilia Moore, moved to Melbourne sometime after his death.

In June 2019 I met with Edward McManus, a significant member of the organising committee behind the Battle of Britain Monument. During the course of collating the names of the participants to feature on the monument, he was relied upon to become familiar with them all through the records available. Today the monument's website provides valuable biographical data, and even photographs, of these airmen; it is a highly useful source of information. With the goodwill, guidance and enthusiasm of Edward McManus, both of whose parents come from Ireland, it was possible to expand the list of Battle of Britain participants with connections to Ireland, and indeed those connected to the wider Irish diaspora, beyond the ten names which are presented on the monument itself under 'Ireland'; it is this enlarged involvement that is presented here in this book.

RAF Fighter Command, symbolically represented in the public mindset by the Spitfire fighter aircraft, in fact possessed far more

Hurricanes than Spitfires; the Hurricane was responsible for 80 per cent of enemy kills during the battle. Defiants, Blenheims and the airmen who crewed them also played their part. Fleet Air Arm Gladiators and Fairey Fulmars were involved, too. It also has to be remembered that there were far more RAF men and women on the ground than in the air; specialists of all kinds supported the airmen: ground maintenance crew, technicians, armourers, airfield defence, the RAF Police, the fire service and a host of others. And then there was Fighter Command itself, its own staff and those of the radar stations, anti-aircraft batteries, barrage balloons, the Royal Observer Corps and, eventually, air-sea rescue. The defence of Britain's air space was multi-faceted and heavily populated.

Perhaps then, many of the myths ought to be seen for the fables that they were, and none more so than that there was little or no Irish contribution of note. There was, and this book is an acknowledgement of that truth. This book, for the first time, presents a fuller indication of the participation of those who have a connection to Ireland, whether they were born, educated, lived or had descendants on the island, or indeed were part of the wider Irish diaspora. The Irish were on the beaches at Normandy on D-Day; they were at the bridge at Arnhem during Operation Market Garden; they crossed the Rhine to engage in the final Battle of Berlin. They were in the cockpits with Fighter Command during the Battle of Britain.

ACKNOWLEDGEMENTS

One unavoidable facet of the Battle of Britain, strategically and tactically, was a consideration of time and space. How to act according to its advantage was crucial to the battle's course and development. The boundless expanse of the airspace over Britain's landmass, in terms of its length, breadth and height, was in fact curtailed by this consideration.

Strategically, the English Channel, the body of water between southern England and Nazi-occupied northern France, was an obstacle to be negotiated, one which severely obstructed the German army's progress to outright victory over all of Europe. Here, the German Wehrmacht (the army) were forced to halt. The time lost taking this 'operational pause' was of significance, as the delay slowed their momentum and granted the RAF vital time and breathing space with which to better prepare and organise.

The distance between German airfields in northern France and Belgium and target areas in southern England, eventually to include London, had important ramifications. Flight time and the Germans' ability to engage in aerial combat was curtailed, as their fighter aircraft and bomber formations were limited by their fuel-carrying capacity.

The seasons and their encompassing weather, including the

duration of daylight and its tidal influences, further limited favourable conditions for invasion. Opportune circumstances were only ever a transient opportunity to be seized upon. The pressure of time was paramount.

In June 1940, however, considerations of such circumstances were far back in the minds of a supremely confident, numerically superior, yet-to-be-defeated Luftwaffe, who were eager for action. Meanwhile the RAF, much more cognisant of the effects of defeat, were acutely mindful of matters of time and space and how they might affect the situation they were facing. Given their scarcity of fighter aircraft and the vast area to defend, they were earnest in considering how best to avoid occupying empty air spaces. They desperately needed to know when, in what direction and strength, and at what height, enemy bomber formations were approaching, and how the best use of time and space could be employed to defend against them.

They had already made good use of time, readying themselves for the inevitable air battle by developing radar and organising the division of the air space in which the battle would be fought. The marshalling of this geographically structured fighter defence system granted a sophisticated, unprecedented framework. The production of fighter aircraft and the training of pilots was crucial, increasing the chances of interception with minimum scramble times. Significantly, these arrangements were not in an effort to counter one big effort over the Channel; instead it was a battle to occur steadily over time. It involved the careful attrition of the Luftwaffe while keeping British losses to a minimum. Such losses were unavoidable, however, and, with the battle ongoing, the time it was taking to train RAF replacement pilots was becoming increasingly crucial. It became a race against time, a competition with the clock which governed the

RAF's ability to reduce the strength of the Luftwaffe before they themselves ran out of pilots.

Thus, time and space played their part in shaping the course of the Battle of Britain – much as they did in the writing of this book. Deadlines and schedules, both the author's and the publisher's, had to coincide to make the publication possible. Also of tantamount importance was the input of Edward McManus of the Battle of Britain Monument Committee; his comprehensive knowledge of the battle's RAF participants was central to its completion. His enthusiasm, graciousness and goodwill in sharing this information was crucial. So was his review of the text in its formative stages, and his unstinting advice and assistance. Thanks also to Maurice Byrne, whose prompt and positive response to my queries was a huge reassurance; to Paul Fry Brigadier General (retired), former General Officer Commanding Irish Air Corps, for writing the foreword for this book, a significant addition; to Conor Graham, Fiona Dunne, Patrick O'Donoghue, Myles McCionnaith and Maeve Convery at Merrion Press; to Deirdre Maxwell, for the typing of the handwritten manuscript; and to Paul O'Flynn, for all his encouragement and practical assistance throughout.

1
SCRAMBLE

The sun shone with a soft quivering light through the seemingly translucent trees. Soon the mood altered and became one of challenge; one of daring and dread. Both militarism and apprehension hung in the air. Moral strength, fortitude and determination were required in responding to the threat of German bombing raids. Such character was evident throughout No. 65 Squadron at RAF Hornchurch in Essex, in late July 1940, not long after the Battle of Britain began.

One among them was Dubliner 'Paddy' Finucane. Brendan Eamonn Fergus Finucane was born in Dublin on 16 October 1920. In 1936, at the age of 16, he moved with his family from Dublin to Richmond in England. He joined the RAF as a trainee pilot in April 1938 and qualified as a fighter pilot flying the Supermarine Spitfire.

The pilots and crew at Hornchurch airfield held no illusions about what the day might hold and they sat poised to go skyward when called. Each coped with this oppressive weight in their own way. They had lost comrades over the preceding weeks and were all aware of the dangers, but the human impulse is to shrug off such admissions of fear. Overall the prevailing sense, while subdued, was stoical, resigned and forbearing. Calm and uncomplaining, they found comradeship sufficient insulation against fear. Their nerves were also helped by faith, both in each other and in the supports of the RAF: a warning system which employed the latest technology and was proving invaluable; the Spitfire and Hurricane aircraft, which were a match for the latest German aircraft; and RAF tactics, leadership and discipline, which were measuring up to the task facing them.

Battle-hardened veterans and fresh-faced newcomers, from England, the Commonwealth and beyond, were bound together despite differences in knowledge and skill; they were made ready to confront the German grab for air supremacy which, if successful, would act as a prelude to an invasion of the south coast of England. It was a battle for control of the skies over Britain and the RAF Fighter Command's task was to deny it to the enemy.

To achieve this, getting fighter aircraft into the air as quickly as possible was vital. It was crucial to get off the ground and into the correct position in order to intercept and shoot down German bombers, dive bombers, fighter bombers and fighter aircraft. Only this would dissuade Hitler, Goering and the German High Command from proceeding with their invasion plans. The aerial combat exchanges had been intense and were increasingly frequent. There was a lot at stake and both sides were committed to the fight.

The rising sun on that late July morning in the long, hot summer of 1940 had just risen above the airfield's tree line when the alarm screamed, its shrill sound splitting the air. The standard routine of the duty shift, only just begun, was already splintered, the calm transformed into clamour, with pilots and aircrew surging towards the aircraft in a flat-out sprint. There was an immediate need to get the Spitfires and Hurricanes into motion – a critical race against time. They were scrambled and the time it took to organise themselves had to be pared to an absolute minimum. Hearts pounded and pulses raced; everyone in the airfield experienced different degrees of a heady dizziness. They all tried to come to terms with what was happening in horizons beyond. Why, this time, had the alarm sounded? What was the nature of what awaited them in the sky? What was the danger and what needed to be done to prevent an unfavourable ending?

Pre-rehearsed drills were put into play and emergency positions were taken. The reactions of the pilots and crew had to be right – perfect, in fact – and there was no margin for error or second chances. British lives were at stake. Their minds were clear, however. Uppermost was only one thought: that no one 'Hun' was getting through today.

To achieve this, they had to get the aircraft sky-bound. The pilots had to 'switch on' mentally while the anxious ground crews sought to prepare the aircrafts' engines by quickly connecting an external power supply. This was called a 'Trolley Acc' (Trolley Accumulator) – a two-wheeled, enclosed hand cart containing accumulators, each having a thick cable which plugged in through a flap in the engine cowling; two rechargeable six-or-twelve-volt lead acid batteries provided the power needed. Small and light enough, ground crews were able to move them with little effort. Meanwhile the pilots, having previously placed their parachutes in the cockpit, or on the wings, and who had hung their helmets on the control column or gunsight, were quickly settling into their cockpits. They hurriedly completed the pre-flight instrumentation checks before taxiing on to the airfield proper; they then pushed forward on the throttle, gained engine speed, achieved lift and accelerated off over the near horizon to face whatever was beyond.

2
WAR

Sunday, 3 September 1939 was All-Ireland Hurling Final day at Croke Park, Dublin. During what became known as the 'Thunder and Lightning' final, Cork hurling hero Jack Lynch stepped up to take a free, not far out from the Kilkenny goal. Kilkenny were one point ahead (two goals and seven points to three goals and three points) and all that was needed was for Lynch to casually tap the sliotar (ball) over the bar and bring the game to a replay. In the event, he went for the match-winning goal (three points) only to see his shot saved! A thunderous roar rose up from the ecstatic Kilkenny fans at the same time as a downpour of rain erupted over Croke Park. Meanwhile, war was erupting over Europe.

The Irish Taoiseach (prime minister) Éamon de Valera addressed the Irish people on Radio Éireann that evening, making a special announcement.

> The great European powers are at war again. That this would happen was almost inevitable for a month past. Yet, until a short time ago, there was hope. But now that hope is gone. The people of Europe are thrown into the misery and anguish of war. I do not want to make you anxious but it would

be a great mistake to think that life can go on here just as before – just as if this European conflict is taking place on another planet. Although we are not engaged in this terrible war, it cannot fail to bring upon us severe hardships, but there is no reason why we should be unduly anxious. As long as our people are of the one mind with regard to the national policy to be pursued, we should be able to surmount all our difficulties. United and disciplined, we have nothing to fear. A nation that has survived centuries of suffering has no need to fear or be daunted. I would like, on behalf of our government and of our people as a whole, to offer our profound sympathy to the men and women of all nations in this period of trial and suffering before them.

Hitler's dream of an Aryan-dominated Europe saw him instruct his army to invade Poland. In responding to the gravity of this aggressive act, Britain declared war on Germany. The prior policy of appeasement adopted by British Prime Minister Neville Chamberlain and his government had proved futile against Hitler's expansionist ambitions and his strong desire to see Nazi totalitarianism dominate.

The Wehrmacht swept through Poland using the heretofore unseen Blitzkrieg (lightning war), combining the speed and mobility of tanks, dive bombers and paratroopers in an unprecedented and overwhelming rate of advance which the Poles were unable to defend against. Germany had prepared, fine-tuned (during the Spanish Civil War) and now perfected their war machine. Massive and rampaging, the fascist Nazi regime was whirling itself westwards until finally France, too, had fallen. Only the Channel separated Britain from a similar defeat. Hitler's war machine, modern, well trained, well equipped and well led, seemed invincible, having brilliantly demonstrated its capacity to outfight and overrun the various oppositions in much of Western Europe. Poland, Denmark, Norway, the Netherlands, Belgium and France all fell under the German jackboot. France fell on 25 June 1940 and Hitler cast his eye across the Channel. The British Expeditionary Force (BEF), having become involved in the Battle of France, was forced to retreat and undertake a humiliating evacuation from Dunkirk (Operation Dynamo) from 26 May to 4 June, where it was fortunate not to have suffered annihilation; as it was, they were forced into leaving most of their heavy equipment there. To bring matters to a neat conclusion, a combined operation would need to be undertaken in order to invade Britain in the summer of 1940 and remove them from the war, entirely. The scene was set; the Battle of Britain was beginning. Survival, freedom and democracy were at stake!

3
AIR SUPERIORITY

The single element likely to seriously impede and even prevent the Germans from a successful invasion of southern England had been identified by their military planners. It existed in the third dimension, introduced with the development of flight: it was the British air threat; the RAF's 'fighter shield'. This source of strength was the British Armed Forces' centre of gravity, the capability from which its military force derived its freedom of action, moral and physical strength, and its will to fight. In short, the RAF stood in the way of German victory in Britain, and throughout all of Europe.

Control of the sky, command of the air; the capacity to fly unhindered over the Channel and the southern English landmass would greatly facilitate victory in Germany's intended invasion of Britain.

If Hitler could not achieve control of the air, then the Germans could not provide secure protection for its invasion force. Commanders on the ground now had to consider what was above the battlefield and what effect it would likely have on their operations. It wasn't simply a matter of having air assets of their own – they had to dominate their enemy's assets; they had to render their air threat redundant.

Gaining air superiority over the RAF would allow the German military commanders to shape the future battle space and better succeed in their next step: the sole concentration of all Nazi expansionist forces on the upcoming Eastern Front campaign against Russia. But first there was the present predicament: to quell and conquer an unbowed Britain. Before German land forces could invade selected beaches along the south coast of England, a plan known as Operation Sea Lion (Unternehmen Seelöwe), control of the sky had to be claimed by physical force.

A debate has occurred among historians regarding Hitler's actual intent to invade Britain; some argue that it was a pressure tactic designed to encourage Britain to seek terms without fighting. It may well be, however, that his intentions had always been aggressive. Not only had he plans prepared to invade England, but there existed a plan to invade Ireland, too. In 1946, one year after the war in Europe had come to an end, an Irish American who had fought with the United States Army called to the Irish Consul General in New York and presented him with a set of books and documents dealing with various aspects of Irish life – its history, economy, geography and topography. He had taken these items from the headquarters of the Luftwaffe in Bavaria after it had been captured. What these items amounted to were plans for the invasion of Ireland, known as Fall Grün (Case Green). The Irish military authorities, however, had already known of Germany's specific intentions as far back as 1942 when a similar set of documents 'came into the possession' of the Irish government. The section of the plans entitled 'General Military Estimate' was supported by photographs of important installations and industrial centres. Maps were also prepared, which emphasised the rough terrain of the Irish coastline. The invasion, if ordered, was to take place by sea. Five to six German divisions were to land on a broad front between Cork and Waterford; the area between Cork and Cobh was listed as a specific gateway, described as 'Offering itself especially for the case of a peaceful or completely surprise landing, in which the considerable natural obstacle of the hinterland can be overcome before the development of any strong enemy counter operation.'

Retrospective academic analysis is important in asserting the facts with the support of documentation. It is instructive, over time, to challenge the generally accepted view. This is both healthy and helpful; such arguments can broaden the perspective of how we view historical events. However, it is also constructive to bear in mind the context of the times: what people were faced with, what they believed in, and how this informed their reactions. Historical evidence does not, therefore, necessarily lead to a greatly altered regard for contemporary accounts. It was known that Hitler would have favoured a British capitulation without committing troops; it is also true that he would welcome an 'easy' victory with little fighting effort. From the British perspective, that a ferocious and brutal battle for air superiority had to be fought if sovereignty, freedom and democracy was to be defended is irrefutable. The Battle of Britain – indeed, the Battle of Britain and Ireland – was fought on these grounds.

That the Luftwaffe's drive to secure air superiority had to be deterred is clear; the threat their bombers and fighter formations posed was real. The battle's eventual outcome was a necessary and proud victory, and men from Ireland played a part in this victory.

It should also be borne in mind that Reich Marshal Hermann Goering and the Luftwaffe were confident of securing a victory. After all, they had cleared the skies of all enemy aircraft in the countries they had previously invaded in their expansionist campaign. Everything that had occurred to date was evidence that their winning ways would continue. The German Navy, however, was a little more circumspect and wary of the still-powerful Royal Navy. They correctly believed that it was tactically unsound to progress their invasion plans until permanent command of the air was secured. The Germans constructed new airfields in the Netherlands, Belgium and France in readiness for the encounter ahead. If air superiority was a prerequisite for the invasion of England, then the harsh reality was that they were going to do their best to secure it.

4
OPERATIONAL PAUSE

In *The Memoirs of Field-Marshal the Viscount Montgomery of Alamein, KG* (1958), General Bernard Law Montgomery, or 'Monty', explains how in July 1940, as commander of the 5th Corps, 'Invasion by the Germans was considered to be probable and we were all preparing to meet and defeat it.' Fascinatingly, he also reveals that, a month earlier, as commander of the 3rd Division, he was to train and prepare his division to return to France; this plan was scuppered following the French capitulation. Instead, he was to prepare to seize the Azores; this eventually changed to the Cape Verde Islands and then, interestingly:

> I was told to prepare for the seizure of Cork and Queenstown (Cobh) in Southern Ireland, so that the harbour could be used as naval base for anti-submarine war in the Atlantic. I had already fought the Southern Irish once, in 1921 and 1922 and it looked as if this renewed contest might be quite a party – with only one division.

General Montgomery was to go on and become one of the best-known British army generals of the Second World War, distinctive for his appearance and distinguished for having delivered victory in

North Africa over Rommel at the Battle of El Alamein (October to November 1942). In 1944 he revised the plan for Operation Overlord, the D-Day invasion at Normandy, and was appointed land component commander for the conduct of operations in North-western Europe, in charge of the 21st Army Group. Later, in September 1944, he devised the daring plan for the seizure of a series of bridges, Operation Market Garden, which saw Allied paratrooper divisions used for the first time strategically.

From a family with deep roots in Moville, County Donegal, General Montgomery was a professional and very serious-minded soldier who had seen service in the First World War, where he was decorated (DSO), and shot and left for dead. He returned after the war, determined that the army could do better, only to be posted to 'Rebel Cork'; during the War of Independence (1919–21) as Brigade Major of the 17th Infantry Brigade stationed in Victoria Barracks (now Collins Barracks) where he considered the conducting of operations to be worse than in the Great War. He felt that the vicious IRA ambushes, Black and Tans reprisals and Auxiliary assassinations 'lowered their standards of decency and chivalry' and was happy when the truce came. At the outbreak of the Second World War he commanded a division in France, prior to Dunkirk, and was among the last of the BEF – over 225,000 men – to be brought back across the English Channel.

The last of the BEF were successfully evacuated on 4 June 1940, leaving the Axis Powers in control of the European continent and poised to invade England and Ireland. The Germans took a self-assured halt to regroup after their highly successful race towards the northern French coastline. Here they instituted an operational pause to consolidate their now heavily extended supply lines and plan for the invasion of southern England and Ireland.

Hitler hoped that Britain would seek an armistice, an agreement not to fight. Capitulation, a blockade, bombardment with massive coastal guns or bombing – these were all possible means by which he could avoid having to invade England.

If the early campaign (despite the series of rapid victories) had taken its toll on German forces, the British had received a massive mauling and needed time to reorganise; they needed to draw breath and, more significantly, halt any defeatist attitude that the Germans were invincible.

Young, competent leadership needed to be encouraged and introduced into the command structures. There was a sense of urgency in the need to mount a meaningful defence; the army needed, instead of being left to 'lick its wounds', to train hard in order to fight.

Britain had a powerful navy and a modern, rapidly expanding air force. What's more, the RAF managed to develop its strength during the Phoney War – the lull between Britain and France's declaration of war on 3 September 1939 and the invasion of the Low Countries and France, beginning 10 May 1940. It had, however, lost pilots and aircraft during the Battle of France and so also needed to re-equip its squadrons. Despite this, all in all, the RAF was in reasonable to good shape with 640 serviceable aircraft and 1,103 trained pilots.

In June 1940, via intercepted communications, the British became aware of the possibility of not only a planned German invasion of England, but also the possibility of a German invasion of Ireland. This risked exposing their western flank. Control of Ireland's landmass and valuable ports (Cork, Castletownbere and Lough Swilly) would act as a boon for a German invasion of Britain and would also extend Germany's range over the Atlantic. This potential was perilous to British interests, and so demanded a swift and robust response. In order to better safeguard their defences, they had to either forcefully take control of the Republic of Ireland, or seek its cooperation in countering the threat. The latter course of action was chosen.

This involvement was controversial given the Republic's policy of neutrality and the fact that its independence from Britain was only recently won through force of arms – members of Irish government had been combatants in the revolutionary period. But an agreement was reached and joint military operations were planned in the event of invasion by Nazi Germany. Plan W, as it became known, was very far out of keeping with the strict notion of neutrality – it necessitated rigorous impartiality, or else the neutral rights were forfeit. It has been said that Ireland was neutral during the Second World War, only that it was 'neutral on the side of the Allies' or 'neutral against Germany'; they returned downed Allied airmen, exchanged intelligence and supplied weather reports ahead of the D-Day landings. So it was very much an 'Irish neutrality' – a highly nuanced neutrality, and one not really in keeping with the exact spirit and ideology of what it meant to be neutral proper. It was practical, pragmatic and flexible; an Irish solution to an Irish problem.

Operationally, Plan W centred on Northern Ireland serving as a base for a new BEF which would cross the border to engage with and repel any German invasion force. The British 53rd (Welsh) Division in Belfast would be the designated strike force, manoeuvring by road and rail. Simultaneously, the 61st Division, in a separate operation, would move into County Donegal, securing Lough Swilly for the Royal Navy. The Royal Marines at Milford Haven would provide a brigade at Wexford as a bridgehead for further operations.

German amphibious landings were likely to target Cork, as it was the nearest landfall between Luftwaffe bases in north-western France and Ireland; however, Limerick, Waterford, Westport, Galway, Sligo and Donegal were not to be excluded, and German paratrooper drops and seaplane-borne landings in lakes were also likely.

Ireland had its own particular context – established attitudes and beliefs – and while many people in the state would have likely assisted the British Army, there were those who would seek to capitalise on the situation, seeing England's difficulty as Ireland's opportunity, and would look at a beleaguered Britain and offer their encouragement to Germany. An IRA uprising or campaign of co-ordinated sabotage and disruption in league with the Germans had to be considered. In the event, a number of German agents were parachuted into Ireland to ferment possible unrest, but all were quickly detained. Defence Force Headquarters had to evaluate the risk and responded with resilience to any such threat. On 24 May 1940, General Defence Plan No. 1 emerged. Its issue directed that armed members of the Garda Síochána (the police) place cordons around areas in which IRA actions occurred and assemble all available troops into mobile columns consisting of one or two companies of infantry supported by detachments from the artillery, engineers, signals and medical corps. As soon as hostile activity was reported, the columns would be tasked 'to enter the area concerned and take positive action to destroy the opposition'. These mobile columns were deployed on a command basis as follows:

Southern Command: Three mobile columns situated in Limerick, Tralee and Templemore with a command reserve located between Cork and Fermoy.

Western Command:	Three mobile columns in Athlone, Galway and Sligo/Castlebar with small detachments stationed at Fort Dunree, Malin Head and in Longford.
Eastern Command:	Two mobile columns with a small reserve. This limited deployment was due to the fact that a large number of troops from this command were tasked with performing various security duties in Dublin.
General Reserve:	One battalion group, centred on the 3rd Battalion and based in the Curragh Camp.

Another consideration was that the British might, in such dangerous and uncertain times, prompted by a changing military situation, execute a hostile invasion of Ireland for its own interests, without seeking cooperation from the Irish government. General Defence Plan No. 2 was therefore approved by the Taoiseach on 15 December 1940. The plan was based on the assumption that a British invasion would consist of three main elements:

- A seaborne operation to capture the ports in Cork, Bantry Bay and Shannon Estuary.
- A combined land and sea operation to capture the forts at Lough Swilly.
- A land offensive from Northern Ireland, moving down the east coast, to capture the aerodromes at Baldonnel and Collinstown, followed by all the territory north of the line traced between Dublin, Athlone and Galway (these locations included).

Defence of the ports and containment of the land offensive were no mean countermeasures to have to undertake, especially by an ill-equipped army operating with many limitations.

Following the German invasion of Europe, a 'state of emergency' was declared by the Irish Government on 7 June 1940. Mobilisation of reserves and an expansion of the Defence Forces quickly followed. At the height of 'the Emergency', as it came to be known, in May 1941 the army had swelled in number to almost 41,000 and in June the local Defence (Reserve) Force reached a strength of 106,000. Mobilisation saw the formation of two divisions and two independent brigades. The 1st Division under Major General MJ Costello had its headquarters in Cork while the 2nd Division under Major General Hugo McNeill had its headquarters in Carton House, Maynooth. The independent 5th and 6th brigades were based in the Curragh, County Kildare and in Rincanna (now Shannon Airport), County Clare respectively.

When the Second World War broke out, Ireland was a long way from being in any way able to resist an invasion. The force was hopelessly understrength and supplies were infinitesimal; there was a chronic shortage of armaments, ammunition, anti-tank weapons, aircraft and accommodation. The Department of Finance had previously ignored the army's pleas for increased spending on military resources in view of the threatening international situation. War was looming and, even after its outbreak, with Hitler advancing across Europe, the department still wanted to save money. Declarations of neutrality mattered little to a rampaging German army. It had taken nine months to finally declare a state of emergency. As well as Operation Sea Lion and Case Green, there was Operation Viking Raid, the German plan to invade Northern

Ireland, either separately or both north and south simultaneously. Less likely, but something that could not be ruled out either, was a similar intention stemming from the United States. This was, after all, a time of war. An invasion from a threat, or a number of threats, was felt to be close at hand; the night skies were being watched for German paratroopers and bombers intent on destruction, the sea's horizons for German invasion ships. Despite this looming threat, provision for an Irish defence capability, when it was still possible to acquire, had been neglected.

Ireland's declaration of neutrality was, therefore, an entirely pragmatic response. The government, and de Valera in particular, made a virtue out of necessity, emphasising that Ireland, as a newly independent country, was asserting its autonomy unambiguously. Neutrality, however, could not be achieved by simply declaring it; a country must also be able to preserve its neutrality militarily. Ireland was criticised for its stance; it was accused, in staying out of the war, of failing in its international responsibility. But, pragmatically, the risks of entering the war were far greater than anything the country could contribute to the war effort. The British would love to have reversed the loss of the treaty ports – the ports retained by the British during the First World War but given over in 1938, after the Anglo-Irish Trade War. British Prime Minister Winston Churchill was particularly frustrated over this situation and was not beyond ordering the ports to be taken back by force.

The best that the Republic could hope for at that early stage of the war was to put a weak, if willing, army into the field. Indeed, many favoured the official adoption of guerrilla tactics and there was, throughout the Emergency, a training emphasis on endurance, marksmanship and night work. Many would have felt comfortable conducting an unconventional war, but as a strategy it was not enough. Ireland was faced, however, with having to organise itself for a conventional war, and the fact that so many Irish men and women were prepared, in such circumstances, to fight and die rather than surrender, has not always been fully appreciated.

Despite official neutrality, Ireland was not immune from the effects of the war. Some of the German aircraft that flew over Ireland after dropping bombs on Britain during the early months did not do so as a result of navigational error, or because they were forced out over the Irish Sea by the RAF. It is clear that these aircraft flew over Ireland on photographic reconnaissance missions as part of the preparation for a possible invasion. Over the months and years to follow, a large number of foreign military aircraft violated Irish air space on a regular basis. Approximately 170 foreign aircraft crashed or were forced to land on Irish territory between 1939 and 1945, either from poor weather, damages, running out of fuel or navigational errors. Of these planes, one of the first to crash-land due to navigational error belonged to the Luftwaffe. On 20 August 1940, the Battle of Britain well progressed at this stage, a Focke-Wulf 200 Condor crashed into the slopes of Mount Brandon above the village of Cloghane, County Kerry. The six-man crew were lucky to escape with their lives and were subsequently arrested by the Garda Siochána. Two had suffered injuries during the crash and were taken to St Catherine's Hospital in Tralee; the remaining four were taken under escort to Collins Barracks, Cork. When they arrived at the barracks, the Germans were taken into custody by the military police and locked in a medical hut. An inexperienced officer sought instruction from Defence Forces Headquarters regarding the correct procedure for dealing with such a situation. Having made his report, he is reputed to have asked the following question, 'Do we shoot them or let them go?' Neither of these options was ever seriously considered. In due course they were transferred to the Curragh Camp, County Kildare, where all foreign airmen who landed in Ireland during the Emergency, both Axis and Allied, were interned.

Kurt Kyck was the navigator on the Focke-Wulf 200. He was later to live in County Meath; interviewed some fifty years later, in 1997, he still remembered his time in Collins Barracks.

> Our stay in Collins Barracks was short, some ten days in all, before we were moved to the Curragh Camp. At first we didn't have much contact with the Irish army, then General Costello paid us a personal visit. He made sure our living conditions were made as comfortable as possible and even arranged for the army band to play a selection of music for us outside the building where we were held.

Kurt Kyck and the rest of the crew of the Focke-Wulf 200 were to spend the rest of the war in the Curragh Camp. During their time there they were allowed out on parole to visit the local towns. In the course of one such visit, Kurt Kyck met a young girl from Kildare town named Lilian White and immediately fell in love. After the war Kurt and Lilian were married and set up home in Ireland. Fifty-five German airmen were interned in the Curragh during the war. Seven of them married Irish girls and two married German girls living in Ireland.

Arthur Voight was a crew member of a Heinkel III with a crew of five. After being attacked during a reconnaissance flight over the Irish Sea in March 1941, they had to make an emergency landing on Rostoonstown beach in front of Tacumshin Lake on the Wexford coast. The radio operator had been shot and killed and was later buried in the German War Cemetery in Glencree, County Wicklow. At the end of the war, Arthur Voight, who had been repatriated, had to escape from the Russian-occupied eastern zone of Germany, returning to Ireland to marry in 1952; he had met the Irish woman while interned in the Curragh.

One hundred and sixty-four German seamen were rescued by MV Kerlogue in the Bay of Biscay and detained in the Curragh Internment Camp. German bombs were to fall on different parts of Ireland, including the North Strand in Dublin, Campile, Dundalk, Monaghan, Carlow and the Curragh. The Belfast docks area was badly bombed and de Valera sent fire brigades from south of the border to assist.

Severely hindered by a number of weaknesses, the emergency army deserves to be remembered not so much for what it did as for what it was ready to do. Two main plans of defence were prepared for either a German or British invasion. Areas were identified for bridge demolitions and the blocking of roads, and barriers and blockhouses were erected. Coastal lookout posts were constructed on prominent points around the coast; eighty-three in all. Anti-aircraft assets were concentrated in Dublin and they actually opened fire during the German bombing of North Strand. The 'call to arms' – the search for men to fill the ranks of the emergency army – was a unifying feature of the period, with old civil war foes collaborating in defence of the country. The risks were real and made all the more fragile because of our lack of preparation and investment in defence supplies.

An estimated 120,000 Irishmen joined the British Army, navy and air force during the Second World War; 70,000 from the south and 50,000 from the north. There was the lure of soldiering and adventure, the compulsion not to miss out, the draw of money and family tradition; there was also sheer altruism. Others, while perhaps agreeing with the state's stance on neutrality, felt they needed to do more – they felt the best way to defend Ireland was to halt Hitler.

Meanwhile an estimated 60,000 additional Irishmen and women went to England as civilian employees, working for the Ministry of Aircraft Production and the Ministry of Supply; a further 100,000 worked elsewhere, mainly in the munitions factories. There were many Royal Ordnance munitions factories throughout Britain during the Second World War producing shells, mines, bullets and war materials of every sort. This involved work with high explosives, toxic chemicals and dangerous machinery, so those working there were at serious risk from accidents, losing limbs and sometimes lives. Stories of accidents at munitions factories were not always reported in the press for reasons of wartime security. Those handling sulphur were nicknamed 'Canary Girls' because it sometimes caused their skin to turn yellow and their hair orange. Edward McManus remembers being fascinated as a child by his aunt Margaret Sullivan from County Longford, as she had an empty (dummy) hand grenade on her bedside locker, a memento of her days working in a grenade-making munitions factory. It was this scale of production, this degree of preparation and organisation, that was the mark of Britain's efficient use of the operational pause.

5
SUMMER SKIES

The British air defence system had been readied to locate and intercept enemy aircraft; to detect and destroy them. To trace tiny dots on a radar screen find their source in the skies. Control of the sky took time, resources and method. It involved fighter aircraft production, pilot training and the putting in place of a fighter control system, Fighter Command. All this and more was necessary so that the senior RAF officers could direct the upcoming battle.

Prior to the declaration of war, with Hitler sounding increasingly bellicose and the threat of confrontation emerging from across Europe, in Britain it became clear that a rearmament programme had to be initiated. Politically, however, Prime Minister Neville Chamberlain sought an avoidance of hostilities; a policy of non-aggression was pursued. In September 1938, at the Munich Agreement, this pursuit of appeasement appeared to bear fruit and 'Peace for our time' was proudly announced by Chamberlain on his return. Notwithstanding this declaration, his arrival back to Britain from Berlin saw an acceleration in the rearmament programme and the progression of the still-incomplete radar detection and fighter control systems.

Air Chief Marshal Sir Hugh Dowding, with foresight and determination, spent four years planning and devising innovative tactics, perfecting the potential of radar and honing the effectiveness of Fighter Command. Responsibility lay with him and he treated his role with exacting conviction; he successfully lobbied for the return of fighter aircraft involved in the Battle of France so that they might be ready and available for the battle he thought would shortly follow.

He did not always enjoy the support of politicians, or even of some within the Air Ministry, but he was single-minded about Britain having a sensible and efficient air defence system. Having commanded a squadron during the First World War, he appreciated the demands of aerial combat and understood aerial warfare. Significantly, he fully appreciated the importance of the advances in air technology since that time. Not only that, he also understood the need for innovation – and so he himself introduced something new. That something was the development of an organised structure, both physical and procedural, to fully synchronise his air defence assets to greatest effect. This would allow Britain to meet the upcoming challenges of a modern air battle, when, in 1940, air power came of age.

With the German invasion of Belgium and Holland on 10 May 1940 and Neville Chamberlain's consequent resignation, Winston Churchill became the new prime minister and he appointed Lord Beaverbrook as Minister of Aircraft Production. Air Chief Marshal Sir Hugh Dowding had been seeking, as a matter of urgency, increased production of new fighter aircraft – Hurricanes and Spitfires. Beaverbrook took to the task with vigour and soon the production lines ran seven days a week; thousands of workers, both men and women, many of whom were from Ireland, worked double shifts, manufacturing the required aircraft at double, or even triple, the output within three to four months – a rate of production that, significantly, exceeded of the Germans.

With new technology and an updated methodology of synchronisation, Air Chief Marshal Sir Hugh Dowding had conceived a new and sophisticated framework for RAF Fighter Command called the Dowding System – a radar-based system of early warning, interception and control. Radio direction finding, or radar, was established through a network of some fifty-two radar stations positioned to detect approaching enemy aircraft along the south-western, southern and eastern coastlines. The twenty-two Chain Home stations and thirty Chain Home Low stations (for the detection of aircraft approaching at low level) had highly visible 350-foot lattice masts, so the Germans knew of their existence. Not fully understood by the Germans, however, was its exact capability and how the information detected was channelled via direct landlines to the underground Filter Room at RAF Bentley Priory (the RAF Fighter Command HQ). Here, filter officers would sift through incoming information before passing it on through closed communication circuits to Group HQs, Sector HQs and the nearest appropriate airfields.

Detected information was to be met with a timely response. Approaching enemy formations could be accurately located at some seventy-mile distances (sometimes more, sometimes less – variables included atmospherics, operator skill, the height of raids, echoes from friendly aircraft and natural features). The aim was to have an incoming formation plotted on operation room maps within four minutes of its first observance by a radar operator; from here, a two-minute reaction was initiated – a scramble – in which the nearest appropriate airfield was reach out to, the Hurricanes and the Spitfires were mobilised, and these aircraft quickly located and intercepted the enemy aircraft formations. The Germans underestimated the effectiveness and accuracy of the early warning capability granted by the radar stations; they believed the operators would be unable to distinguish between large and smaller formations – and that the system would not be able to cope with large numbers approaching simultaneously, being made redundant.

As good as they were at detecting the approach of incoming enemy aircraft, once those aircraft had passed over the radar masts, they became invisible to radar. However, by now the Observer Corps was alerted; their purpose was to maintain a visual on the approaching enemy aircraft formations and report their height, bearing and number. The Observer Corps was part of the integrated air defence system, working hand in glove with radar stations and airfields via the newly structured Group and Sector HQs.

At night or in poor visibility (from bad weather), instead of monitoring the enemy aircraft's progress by sight, they would do so by sound, via their network of monitoring posts. By day, a mechanical sighting instrument mounted over a gridded map (a circular representation of the reporting areas for a particular post) called a Post Instrument assisted greatly in the identification and locating of enemy aircraft. These posts were manned mainly by civilians.

Dublin-born General Sir Frederick Pile's father was Sir Francis Thomas Devereux Pile, who served as Lord Mayor of Dublin from 1900 to 1901. Frederick Pile, having served in the First World War, was made General Officer Commanding-in-Chief of the Anti-Aircraft Command at the outbreak of the Second World War, a position which he held, unusually, throughout the entire war – he was the only British general to retain the same command for the entirety of its duration. Anti-Aircraft Command was another integrated element of Britain's air defence system during the Battle of Britain and beyond. Barrage balloon units were placed along routes of enemy aircraft raids. Far from being ineffectual, a line of barrage balloons with trailing cables, some with extra hanging cables to which explosive devices could be added, were a great obstacle for attacking aircraft crewmen when effectively positioned. The great efforts it took to avoid hitting them along defensive perimeters, or throughout a circular area, meant they were a formidable defence method.

Air Chief Marshal Sir Hugh Dowding split the country into four groups, each with its own Group Headquarters (Numbers 10, 11, 12 and 13). In turn, each Group HQ was split into a number of sectors containing fighter airfields. In one of the sectors, there was the Sector Control Station. So it was on the ground below the Group HQs that the Dowding System was set to play out, or not, its defence of Britain in 1940 under summer skies! It was, however, in these summer skies that the fighting would take place.

6
ATTRITION

The ability to fly was a mental faculty. Being able to fly a high-performance fighter aircraft was an aptitude; you either possessed a natural ability or you did not. However, being able to both fly and fight required a further flair – this was a different mental power again. There were those who had a talent for it and this difference was what separated the aces from the rest – many of whom, if they could not measure up in the moment of aerial combat, had to bail out, or crashed. Having the aptitude to make the best use of the aircraft's performance capability, the awareness to see what was going on around oneself, the dexterity of a good shot, and the mental competence and adept courage to overcome fear meant that some even thrived while in flight. Such skill and spirit came to epitomise the character, the plucky determination, of the RAF. It was also, however, the bedrock of the success of the Luftwaffe. Heretofore, it swept all other air forces aside. Their success yielded confidence, a certainty and a belief in themselves. Their aces were poised with a self-assured conviction of their own prowess; they were anxious to project their power, proficiency and skill, and to dominate the skies over Britain. They were also curious, even eager, to experience the coming contest with the Hurricane and Spitfire.

It was a professional inquisitiveness; they were intrigued, not at all reluctant or unsure.

The Battle of France, and especially the British evacuation at Dunkirk, had already pitched, to a certain extent, the RAF and the Luftwaffe against each other. Each was not an entirely unknown entity to the other – and this was also true of their fighter aircraft. Three Spitfires had been captured on the ground, in June, during the fall of France. A month earlier, the British had received a Messerschmitt Bf 109E, which had landed intact in France, in the wrong place due to bad weather, in November 1939. Each side set about examining the other's aircraft type in a series of test flights, mock dogfights and technical evaluations in order to discover the advantages one aircraft may have held over another. An understanding of these advantages made them mindful of the modifications necessary for improvements to later models. It was important information to have, and in the interim, with the Battle of Britain encroaching, it would be interesting to see how the experience of the aerial reality measured up against their respective assessments.

Of course, another important factor were the tactics to be employed and the reasoning behind their choosing. Experience had taught the Luftwaffe to amend their approach to aerial formations. They had learned that the best way to create a surprise aerial ambush (known as a 'bounce') was to dive from a height, from the rear or to come 'out of the sun', using its dazzling brightness to shield their approach. Of course, to engage successfully, you had to see your opponent. Whoever saw the opposition first had an advantage and had better chance of achieving a bounce. In order to better enable them to search the skies, the Luftwaffe abandoned the V-shaped 'Vic' formation, as only the leader was on the lookout for enemy aircraft – the other pilots were intensely concentrating on maintaining the formation shape. Instead, the Luftwaffe used the basic *Rotte* (pair), a leader and wingman; nearly always, however, there were two pairs together in a *Schwarm* (flight). In turn, three *Schwarms* made up a *Staffel* (twelve aircraft) and there were three *Staffels* in a *Gruppe*, some thirty-six fighter aircraft. Add in command and staff aircraft, and a *Gruppe* of between forty and fifty fighter aircraft was ordinarily what took to the skies.

In contrast, the RAF, in Vic formations, consisted of one squadron of twelve fighter aircraft, mostly operating on their own; occasionally two Squadrons operated together, but rarely did it go beyond that. Firepower was the reason for the continuance of the unwieldy Vic formation. The Hurricanes and Spitfires were armed exclusively with rifle calibre .303" machine-gun ammunition and their firepower, when attacking independently, was insufficient to bring down a German bomber. In order to make the most of the firepower available, it was important to mass together in close formation, concentrating their destructive effect.

Trained pilots, technologically advanced fighter aircraft and concerted tactics were all going to have their effect on the outcome of the battle, and, as it developed, other elements would also influence matters. However, the principal strategy employed on both sides was one of attrition, the wearing away of attack and defence.

The Luftwaffe would 'offer' tightly packed bomber formations over the Channel as targets to draw out the British fighter aircraft and then attack them with their own, thereby depleting the RAF stock over time. The intention was to bring this to a point where the defenders would have little or no fighter aircraft left with which to prevent the amphibious invasion of southern England.

The British, for their part, wished to engage the German bombers with their Hurricanes; to do this, they used their Spitfires to attack and draw off the German fighter escorts first. In turn, this caused the loss of both German bombers and fighters.

The Battle of Britain was to be a battle of attrition. It was to be a fiercely contested struggle, where the defenders, Irishmen among them, fought for survival and freedom. The scene was set for an enthralling encounter – the actuality surpassing expectation.

7

PHASE ONE – CONFLICT COMMENCED

The three-and-a-half-month epic encounter – the Battle of Britain – saw five distinct periods over which the course of the aerial conflict changed and developed, ebbed and flowed, as events both planned and unplanned unfolded. Phase One (26 June–16 July) saw the conflict commence with scattered and limited day and night attacks, mainly directed against shipping and coastal towns.

The Luftwaffe's concept of attrition was Blitzkrieg. In other words, annihilation. And they had 2,800 aircraft to do it with – two thirds of which were bombers. In early July they more consciously attacked coastal convoys in the Channel to cut off British supply lines, but the principal intention was to come into contact with British fighter aircraft, which they then hoped to decimate with their greater numbers. Hitler hoped this belligerent posturing would encourage Churchill and the British government to sue for peace; while they were making up their mind, his Luftwaffe would reduce the RAF's fighter capability. The Battle of Britain was already a battle of wits as much as a battle of will.

In any event, it was not only the Luftwaffe that were full of confidence. Hitler himself was buoyant after the fall of France and a certain boundless bravado prevailed among the whole of the

German army. It had most certainly gotten a purchase on the psyche of Goering, head of the Luftwaffe, who was full of bluster, bragging that the fall of Britain would only be a matter of days. From late June, intermittent day and night raids were commenced by the Luftwaffe. These attacks included the laying of naval mines; they were directed, for the most part, against ports along the southern coast and shipping convoys in the Channel, though some aircraft factories were also targeted from the air. So with hostilities against Britain already under way, albeit scattered and limited, it can be asserted – and is maintained by a number of historians – that the Battle of Britain had already begun.

Hitler was ordering preparatory invasion plans and oscillating in his considerations of how much pressure to put on the British in order to secure their capitulation. Aerial exchanges were under way, shots were being fired, and death and destruction was already a reality. The Luftwaffe were successful in provoking a response from the RAF, but the RAF's reaction was well prepared, systematic and technologically advanced – and they had the home advantage.

The Dowding System demarcated the country into four groups as a means of better commanding it. 11 Group, in the south-east, was geographically positioned to witness most of the action, and half of the total fighter aircraft strength was placed there; it was under the command of New Zealander Air Vice Marshal Keith Park and its HQ was located at RAF Uxbridge, Middlesex. 10 Group was positioned in the south-west and was under the command of Air Vice Marshal Sir Quintin Brand; its HQ was located at RAF Box, Wiltshire. 12 Group, positioned in the Midlands and in the east, was under Air Vice Marshal Trafford Leigh-Mallory; its HQ was located at RAF Watnall, Nottinghamshire. 13 Group were positioned to respond to action from Yorkshire to Scotland and across to Northern

Ireland – a huge area, but at a remove from the main battleground. It was under the command of Air Vice Marshal RE Saul and its HQ was located at RAF Kenton in Tyne and Wear. This was a reserve area from which to give depth to the defence but also to rotate 'fresh' squadron pilots into 11 Group's area of responsibility while receiving exhausted airmen, for a duration, to allow them to rest up and recharge their energy levels.

The RAF pilots belonging to Fighter Command squadrons were a mixed group, mostly from Britain and Commonwealth countries, but also from a variety of other countries, whether allied or not. The pilots themselves were a combination of career pilots who joined during the early to mid-1930s, those called up as reservists (RAF Volunteers Reservists – RAFVR) and those granted short-term commissions who underwent basic flying courses at flight training school and at the Operational Training Units (OTUs). Many had to do conversion courses to fly the Hurricane, the Spitfire and the Blenheims.

From Ireland there were men like Georges Jacques Grogan, born on 24 October 1909, who joined the RAF as an aircraft apprentice in September 1926, qualifying in August 1929. He served overseas throughout the 1930s in places like Northern Kurdistan, India and the north-west frontier. At the outbreak of war, he volunteered for aircrew duties. He was commissioned in January 1940 and in February he joined 23 Squadron at Wittering as an air gunner. He served in, and survived, the Battle of Britain and was posted abroad in March 1941. He survived the war and stayed on in the RAF after the war, retiring in November 1956 as a squadron leader. He died in 1983.

William Winder McConnell, born in Belfast on 9 June 1917, joined the RAFVR in February 1939 as an airman under training (u/t) pilot and began his flying training at a reserve flight training school in Belfast before being called up on 1 September 1939, the day that Germany invaded Poland. He attended flight training school at Little Rissington and on completion was to report to an OTU. He was, however, then told to join 245 Squadron at Hawking, arriving on 18 June 1940 with two others. None of the three could fly Hurricanes. Pilot Officer W.W. McConnell was to see service with 32 Squadron (Acklington), 607 Squadron (Tangmere) and 249 Squadron (North Weald) during the Battle of Britain.

McConnell survived the Battle of Britain but in January 1941 he was bounced by a Messerschmitt 109 over the Channel and received a bullet wound in his left leg. He managed to turn towards the English coast and bailed out over Dover, being picked up by an air-sea rescue (ASR) launch; his Hurricane went head on into the white cliffs. It is thought likely that another Irishman, Wing Commander Victor Beamish from West Cork (Dunmanway), destroyed McConnell's attacker. McConnell recovered after four months and was awarded the Distinguished Flying Cross (DFC) in June 1942. He became Squadron Commander of 174 Squadron and received a bar to the DFC in September 1942. In February 1944, on a long-range sweep over France while flying a Typhoon, he was forced to crash land due to a fuel leak from a main tank. He landed near the village of Percy, south of Saint-Lô, was captured by the Germans, and was imprisoned in Stalag Luft III and Milag Nord at Tarmstedt, where he sat out the rest of the war. Released from prison, and subsequently the RAF, in December 1945, the following year, in October, he joined Aer Lingus as a pilot and served with them for thirty years, after which he did one year with Zambian Airlines, before retiring in 1977. He died in 1998.

Three Belfast RAFVR men, Noel Henry Corry, Robert Ronald Wright and Victor Hall Skillen, were called up to full-time service after the outbreak of the war and converted to flying Blenheims. As did William Storey Moore, the 'Australian' from Dublin, only he joined on a short service commission. They served with 25, 248, 29 and 236 squadrons, respectively. Right from the war's commencement, the Blenheim were slower and less manoeuvrable than the RAF Spitfire and Hurricanes, and so fared badly against the faster Luftwaffe fighters, especially the Messerschmitt Bf 109. In the Battle of France they suffered high losses, attacked by ground-based anti-aircraft flak and from enemy fighters in the skies. Three squadrons of Blenheims from Coastal Command were augmented by those already in Fighter Command and these then became deployed in the night fighting role. Night fighting was different to day fighting insofar as it involved 'stalking' the enemy in order to get into firing position without being observed. The aircraft engaged in stalking would approach from below – the better to spot and identify the aircraft as enemy. Once they had confirmed that the other aircraft was not a 'friendly' they would regulate their speed to that of the other aircraft; then, rising slowly behind the enemy aircraft, keeping below their slipstream, they would proceed close to them (a maximum range of 150 yards) and open fire, bringing a satisfactory conclusion to their night interception sortie.

The three Belfast men and Moore survived the Battle of Britain. However, neither Victor Skillen nor William Moore survived the war. Noel Corry converted to Wellington bombers and was awarded the DFC in December 1944. He was released from the RAF in November 1945 as a squadron leader. He died in March 2006.

Robert Wright spent most of the Battle of Britain conducting long-range sorties to Norway on the lookout for the supposed

German invasion fleet. Commissioned in January 1941, he moved to 248 Squadron at Brize Norton and attacked E-boats off the Dutch coast having converted to, and later instructed on, Beaufighters (the Blenheim replacement). He joined 235 Squadron at Leuchars and carried out long-range fighter patrols over the Bay of Biscay, protecting anti-submarine aircraft from German fighters. He shot down a Junkers 290 on 16 February 1944 and was awarded the DFC in April 1944. He also shot down a Junkers 88 on 9 June and later converted to Mosquitos. Released from the RAF in December 1945 as a squadron leader, he returned to work for Avery, the scale manufacturer, and retired in 1982. He died in 1997.

All those mentioned in this chapter were in uniform. They were in aircraft from the preliminary phase of the Battle of Britain and were to be involved in operations, action and kills throughout the coming phases of the battle.

One of those directing them and others towards these 'kills' was Group 11's Biggin Hill Controller, Squadron Leader Bill Igoe from Nenagh Co. Tipperary son of an RIC man. Educated at Presentation College Bray he went on to study Engineering in University College Cork. This in turn led to a scholarship to the London College of Aeronautical Engineering which was the ideal pathway into the RAF, where he became first a fighter pilot and then a Flying Boat Captain in RAF Wittering with 29 (F) Squadron. After a posting to Egypt in 1935 he found himself back in Britain at RAF Biggin Hill one year later, and from there went to 213 Squadron in Northolt. On 12 April 1937 Bill Igoe was involved in a flying accident which resulted in a six-month hospitalisation to recover from serious third-degree burns. On the outbreak of the war he reported to Biggin Hill and became a highly successful Controller in which role, all throughout the summer of 1940 he excelled, seeming to have an innate grasp of radar and how to meaningfully interpret, quicker and more accurately than most, the indications its radio waves were detecting. Post Battle of Britain, in 1943 he went on to Command RAF Beachy Head as a specialist in radar development for use with Fighter Control. He survived the war and went on to have a highly successful business career in Africa. A gifted sportsman with rugby, boxing, tennis and swimming among his involvements, he was professionally very able, educated, and amenable. His contribution during the Battle of Britain, like so many other Irish, in the air and on the ground, was an important one. British Prime Minister Winston Churchill was often quoted as saying Britain 'stood alone' in the Summer of 1940; it was not however without the significant individual contributions of others, from many countries, Ireland among them.

8

PHASE TWO – STATE OF ALERT

Phase Two (17 July–12 August) began to raise a state of alert. There were larger and more frequent Luftwaffe attacks against shipping in the English Channel, ports along the south and east coasts, and RAF facilities and towns with aircraft factories.

Friday, 19 July 1940. Hitler's rhetoric filled the Reichstag (the German Parliament) in Berlin. Hundreds of miles to the west, nine RAF Defiants from 141 Squadron were involved in aerial combat with twelve Messerschmitt Bf 109s off Dover. The unequal exchange was over in minutes and six Defiants were downed. Air Gunner Sergeant Albert Curley, 33 years old, from Bushey, Hertfordshire, but born in Ballincollig, County Cork, crashed into the Channel along with his Defiant L6995 and the pilot. Both men were reported lost. Three days previously, losing patience with Churchill, Hitler had issued his 'Directive 16', ordering that planning and preparations be stepped up for a landing in England. But first the RAF had to be reduced to a degree that it would be incapable of adversely affecting the German crossing of the Channel. The Defiant fighter aircraft had a crew of two – a pilot and a gunner in a separate turret – however, they were vulnerable from both below and head on, and the Luftwaffe had been quick to spot this. Albert's father

John had been stationed in Ballincollig, County Cork, with the 6th Dragoons, and had taken part in the South African campaigns and in Egypt during the First World War. He later returned to Ireland with the Auxiliary Division of the Royal Irish Constabulary. Albert Curley had joined the RAFVR in May 1939 and was called up to full-time service in September, whereupon he trained as an air gunner and went to serve with 141 Squadron in June 1940. A month later he was killed. After its deadly encounter, what was left of the squadron was withdrawn to Scotland. Defiants, henceforth, were considered unusable as daytime fighters. Their development and deployment as night fighters proved more successful; thirteen such squadrons were put into service.

This phase of the developing battle saw larger and more frequent daylight attacks against merchant shipping convoys in the Channel – around coastal ports along the eastern seaboard and the southern shorelines. Night attacks also developed; they took place from the east coast, through the midlands, to the west, with RAF facilities and the aircraft industry being targeted. Leading up to this phase, and during it, RAF squadrons were being called into action at an increasing rate and newcomers from Fighter Command had been receiving their first taste of aerial combat. They had inflicted 'kills' on the enemy and in turn sustained losses of their own, both aircraft and pilots. Attacks on merchant convoys and the ports of Dover were most prevalent, but Plymouth and Portsmouth also received close attention from German bombing raids. The pressure was intensified and the air assaults were more acute, with the result that the air fighting became fiercer. Fighter Command found itself equal to the challenge, but there were days when front-line aircraft, especially in 11 Group, had to be supplemented. Defiants were deployed from their base at West Malling in order to meet this demand, only they proved no match for the far faster, more manoeuvrable Messerschmitt fighters. However, the RAF Hurricane and Spitfire fighters were also having their successes, and in the fortnight leading up to the commencement of this phase, sixty-seven German aircraft had been shot down while the RAF had only lost twenty-six. Only now the attacks were considerably more substantial and sustained. Weather managed to interrupt the now daily bombardments, bringing some measure of relief to the otherwise increased pressure from the Luftwaffe.

Prior to this point, the Luftwaffe had been largely unimpeded in their westward advance through the skies of Europe. They had suffered casualties, particularly in the Battle of France, but they now occupied newly created airfields along the northern French coastline and in Belgium, and they were large in numbers with high morale. The RAF proved formidable opponents, despite this. They enjoyed the distinct advantage of radar, their fighter aircraft were on a par with the Luftwaffe, and they didn't have to fly over the Channel to engage in combat. Radar detected German bomber and fighter escort formations as they built up over France and Belgium; once lost to radar, the Observer Corps plotted their height, course and number through sight, sometimes with single 'Joe Crow' aircraft observers in the sky confirming information. Would the RAF or the Luftwaffe prevail? Death and destruction were being delivered by both sides.

Harold Arthur 'Jim' Fenton, a doctor's son, was born in Argentina, brought up in County Sligo, and educated at Sandford Park School and Trinity College Dublin. He became squadron leader of 238 (Hurricane) Squadron. When appointed to command the squadron in June 1940, he had only fifteen hours of operational experience, and even those were in a Spitfire. During this phase of the battle, with shipping in the Channel subject to intense attacks, 238 Squadron, like those across 11 Group, was scrambled repeatedly. On one such day, 8 August, a prolonged, intense Luftwaffe attack on a Royal Navy-escorted merchant convoy codenamed 'Peewit' resulted in a protracted and costly aerial exchange, during which 238 Squadron downed four enemy aircraft (two Messerschmitt 109s and two Messerschmitt 110s) and damaged a third Messerschmitt 109 – all for the loss of two Hurricanes.

Going low level, just above the Channel's surface, seeking survivors, 'Jim' Fenton spotted a German Heinkel 59 seaplane, which he immediately engaged. His attack was successful, but he and his aircraft were hit in the exchange and he was forced to ditch his Hurricane in 'the drink'. Escaping from the cockpit before he sank with his aircraft, his parachute came loose. Fortunately, it floated and he used it to maintain buoyancy until he was picked up by an armed convoy escort trawler. Returning to dry land, he shared the skipper's cabin with a rescued German pilot. He was hospitalised for a duration, during which the squadron became depleted, reduced to only five serviceable aircraft. On his return he set about reconstituting his squadron's aircraft numbers and his efforts were rewarded with the arrival of eight replacement Hurricanes. The newly strengthened squadron took up the fight in earnest. Before the battle was over, he himself had destroyed a German Dornier 17 Bomber and a Messerschmitt 110 fighter. He survived both the Battle of Britain and the war, and died aged 86.

Ground radar was playing its part; its integration into Fighter Command's fighter control system was reaping rewards and greatly assisting in the fight for air superiority over southern England. Airborne radar was also being pioneered by the RAF and the Blenheim aircraft possessed the internal space required to house the new Airborne Interception radar (AI). On the night of 21 July it was first successfully used in shooting down a Dornier 17. Some ten days later, Sergeant Joseph Beckett Thompson, 24 years old, of Magheragall, Northern Ireland, piloting a Blenheim during a further test of the AI radar system, was unfortunately involved in a mid-air collision with another Blenheim aircraft over the Bristol Channel. All six aircrew died.

Two days after Hitler's address in the Reichstag, Dublin-born Pilot Officer Brian Bertram Considine, flying a Hurricane with 238 Squadron (whose Squadron leader was 'Jim' Fenton) out of Tangmere, claimed the destruction of a German Messerschmitt 110 fighter. His family came from Limerick, however, at the time of his birth, his father, a doctor, was governor of the criminal lunatic asylum in Dundrum, Dublin. Joining the RAFVR in December 1938 as an airman u/t pilot, he was called up at the outbreak of the war, and, after completion of his training in 3 Flight Training School Grantham in November 1939, he went to 6 OTU Sutton Bridge in May 1940 to convert to Hurricanes. Posted to 236 (8) Squadron, he fought throughout the Battle of Britain and on 27 August, with his squadron leader, he intercepted a Dornier bomber over Plymouth, causing damage to its starboard engine, disabling it and forcing it to belly-land at Tavistock in Devon. Surviving the battle, he himself was shot down five days after its 'official' ending. Despite wounds, he managed to bail out as his aircraft descended and crashed. He spent the remainder of the war flying in and around the Middle East and was subsequently released from the RAF. He flew for four years with Aer Lingus before going into advertising. He died in 1996.

The RAF, and the Irishmen who belonged to its ranks, fought hard, fought well and, with 'systemised' assistance from Fighter Command, fought cleverly. Air Chief Marshal Sir Hugh Dowding and Air Vice Marshal Keith Park had steadfastly refused to allow their squadrons to become embroiled en masse, which is what the Luftwaffe had hoped would happen – they wanted to lure the RAF fighters out in large numbers and then, with their own overwhelming numbers, to destroy them. Instead, guided by radar and directed by Fighter Command, one squadron, occasionally two, rarer still three, took on the superior numbers of German bomber and fighter formations, whittling down their numbers according to their own terms. As the weeks passed, the aerial actions were taking their toll on both sides – the Luftwaffe continuously losing more aircraft than the RAF.

Early August witnessed an unusually poor spell of weather for that time of year and, although Luftwaffe sorties continued, there was a perceptible decrease in air activities. There was, however, no cutback in the production of replacement fighters and the repairs made to damaged aircraft. Fighter aircraft were available to the RAF, but pilots were not so easily replaced; this was a serious source of concern for Fighter Command, because they knew, over the coming weeks, they were going to need them badly.

9

PHASE THREE – A DECISIVE VICTORY DEMANDED

Phase Three (13 August–6 September) commenced when the Luftwaffe, realising that their tactics were not yielding results, changed their objective, seeking to exhaust the RAF's defences and claim a decisive victory with large-scale daylight attacks against RAF airfields in the south-east of England.

The German bomber formations were located by radar; their progress was tracked and their flightpaths plotted by the Observer Corps; their intent was thwarted by RAF fighter interception. The battle was not going quite as the Luftwaffe imagined it would. German bomber and fighter aircraft losses were mounting. Luftwaffe fighter pilots felt aggrieved that they were not allowed by the Supreme Commander of the Luftwaffe, Hermann Goering, to fight the battle on their own terms; 'dead engines', aircraft running out of fuel whilst aloft, were becoming all too frequent an occurrence, forcing many to disengage from combat and struggle to stay airborne while crossing back over the Channel. One third of the 400-litre capacity of the Messerschmitt 109 fighters was being used up in the time it took to rendezvous and form up with the bombers, before the bombing raids had properly begun.

Having to stay near to the bombers while providing 'close' or 'indirect' escort, the fighters also had to reduce their flying speed to match that of the bombers. 'Free Chase' was largely denied to them – the natural state of being for a Luftwaffe fighter pilot, employing the elements of speed and manoeuvrability to good effect. Instead, protection of the slower-moving, more cumbersome bomber formations was given priority.

For the RAF fighter pilots, Fighter Command unleashed their squadrons in a controlled, cohesive manner, mindful of the bigger tactical picture. They sometimes managed to intercept from a height, hit the bombers and were gone. At others, the Luftwaffe's escorting fighters provided a defence; resistance resulted and dogfights occurred. The RAF, too, were losing fighter aircraft and pilots.

Aware that the penetration of the Luftwaffe fighters was constrained by fuel consumption, the RAF sometimes waited until the Luftwaffe were well inland before offering battle, knowing that this adversely affected the ability of the Luftwaffe to engage fully in aerial combat. If tactically sound, they also attacked them as they headed back over the Channel, very low on fuel. As the battle took place over Britain, any downed RAF airmen that bailed out and came to ground uninjured could be back in the fight in hours; the Luftwaffe pilots, faced with similar circumstances, were brought to a prisoner-of-war camp, and it was the end of the war for them.

Matters could not continue in this way. A decisive victory over the RAF had been demanded and the current scheme of aerial manoeuvring was not going to achieve that end. Goering realised that he needed to change his point of attack. Unable to achieve the necessary rate of destruction of RAF fighters, he decided to destroy them at source instead: on the ground, at their airfields. To do this, he sent an enlarged and more focused Luftwaffe force over the

Channel. Adlertag ('Eagle Day'), on 13 August 1940, was the first day of Unternehmen Adlerangriff ('Operation Eagle Attack'); on this day, sorties of far larger formations were deployed in swarms to destroy RAF fighter aircraft and airfields, especially those of 11 Group in south-east England. These more intensive, large-scale daylight attacks against RAF airfields and Fighter Command installations had the objective of exhausting, if not entirely extinguishing, the RAF's ability to provide a defence. Nor were night attacks to be discontinued. The targets were changed, the tempo increased – for the Germans, the time for victory was now because the timetable for invasion demanded it. The Battle of Britain had entered a new and deadly phase. Indeed, some historians regard Adlertag as the actual commencement of the Battle of Britain.

The RAF's fighter control system was about to receive its most severe test to date. Would its physical infrastructure remain intact? Could it maintain its operational cohesion? Would its command and control structure become swamped, even overwhelmed? Would the Luftwaffe's new initiative render the RAF 'fighter shield' redundant?

Early on 13 August, as soon as the Women's Auxiliary Air Force (WAAF) plotters in the Fighter Command Operations Room at Bentley Priory began moving the markers around on the general situation map, it became apparent to the duty controller that something new and unusual was occurring. He was responsible for allocating incoming raids to the most appropriate RAF group and, in order to meet the various threats, he had to order an ever-increasing number of responses. It was to be the same case for several of the days that succeeded; over the Channel, the hugely enlarged Luftwaffe bomber and fighter formations came in successive waves, early and often. The skies were never fuller; the German air armada was never more threatening.

All of this had not been put into action without prior preparation. Radar installations and coastal fighter stations were targeted in the days leading up to Adlertag, particularly on 8 and 12 August. Damage was done and buildings were destroyed, but, ironically, the large, 350-foot radar masts proved difficult to obliterate, as did the underground lines and communications network that connected Fighter Command to its fighter control system. So, while it was a lot more hectic and unnerving, the RAF's infrastructure was largely unscathed and continued much as before, only with greater urgency.

The intensification of Luftwaffe raids, now targeting RAF airfields, did result in bombardments which destroyed hangars, buildings and runways, and resulted in injury and loss of life. As airmen from 11 Group were being scrambled to intercept the seemingly ever-increasing numbers of Luftwaffe formations, squadrons from 10 and 12 groups were scrambled to protect the very airfields from which 11 Group had taken off from. With more Luftwaffe aircraft in the air and more RAF fighter squadrons sent to meet them, there was more destruction and loss.

For some, however, this occasion meant that their moment had come. On 12 and 13 August, Brendan 'Paddy' Finucane, from Dublin, of 65 Squadron at Hornchurch, claimed two Messerschmitt 109s – two probables and one damaged. For someone whose rate of progress as a trainee pilot was patchy and rated 'below average', he, like others, rose to the challenge when it was demanded. Though his flying instructor may not have extended the same courtesy to others of his skill level, Finucane's determination had impressed his instructor enough to allow him to progress. Now, at the height of the battle, Finucane was demonstrating his characteristic determination, though now he added an exceptional flair, both for flying and fighting.

Hill Harkness, from Belfast, was also successful in downing German aircraft. He took command at RAF Northolt in July and, on 12 August, he 'probably' destroyed a Dornier 17 medium bomber, nicknamed the 'flying pencil' due to its slim fuselage. The following day, on Adlertag, he shared in the destruction of a Junkers 88 'Wunderbomber', a high-speed medium bomber that could also perform as a dive bomber. Harkness survived both the battle and the war; he died in April 2002.

Not so lucky was Cecil Robert Montgomery, 26 years old, from Lisnashea, County Fermanagh. He flew a Hurricane with 615 Squadron when, on 14 August, he was reported as missing after combat over the Channel, off Dover; his Hurricane had crashed into the sea. His body was subsequently washed up on the French coast. He is buried in Oye-Plage Communal Cemetery.

Also in action on 14 August, and from County Fermanagh, was Henry William Beggs, 23 years old, from Irvinestown. He had joined the Fleet Air Arm and was attached to the RAF in mid-June 1940; he converted to Hurricanes and joined 151 Squadron at Martlesham Heath on 1 July. He destroyed a Messerschmitt 109 on 14 August, but was shot down the following day while in combat with Messerschmitt 109s over Dover; he crashed at Shorncliffe and was wounded. He returned to the Fleet Air Arm (883 Squadron) after the Battle of Britain, but was lost when HMS *Avenger* was sunk by a U-boat while returning to the Clyde from the landings in North Africa in mid-November 1942.

While wounded after his crash at Shorncliffe, he, like other injured pilots, may well have been attended to by an Irish nurse, as there were many Irish nurses in hospitals in wartime London and elsewhere. One such nurse was Mary Morris, formerly Mulry, from Caltra, County Galway. Morris was trained in Guy's

Hospital in London and was transferred to Kent after training. Her nursing duties included caring for survivors following the Dunkirk evacuation and reviving injured pilots from the Battle of Britain. Details of this and her later nursing career are contained in her diary, which is held in the Imperial War Museum and was published in 2014 as *A Very Private Diary: A Nurse in Wartime*. Her brother Michael emigrated to the US, fought with the US forces on D-Day, and went on to enter and liberate Buchenwald concentration camp in Germany.

Another Irish woman, Eileen (Eil) McSweeney, born in 1916, left her home in Ballydehob, County Cork, in her late teens and trained as a nurse in Bethnal Green Hospital in the East End of London. She remained there throughout the Battle of Britain, the Blitz and beyond. She undertook a qualification in child welfare during the course of her studies and was presented with her graduation medal in Guy's Hospital London in 1940, a year of intense aerial bombardment on the English capital.

The frequent wailing of warning sirens, termed 'the wailing cow', was, in the very least, a source of irritation, as everyone would have to drop what they were doing immediately and scurry for the nearest underground station, for those in their homes, or for the Anderson air-raid shelter in their gardens. Designed in 1938 and named after Sir John Anderson, Home Secretary during the Battle of Britain, these sanctuaries were dug into gardens and covered over with displaced earth; though people inside could feel the ground shake from explosions, they provided a degree of protection from shell splinters and bomb fragments. They could accommodate up to six people and the government supplied them for free to low income families – the wealthier families having to pay for theirs. One and a half million Anderson shelters were distributed in the months before the outbreak of the war and, in all, 3.6 million were produced before production ended.

Whilst on night duty, the nurses in Guy's Hospital would knit thick socks for the 'boys on the naval boats'. Great care was taken to turn the heel, keeping the stitches tight with thoughts of their cold damp conditions. When a sailor finally made it onto the wards, he was eagerly asked how much he appreciated this wartime effort. He replied that he had indeed received socks and commented how useful they were to stop draughts in the portholes. 'Eil' had a lot of stories about soldiers sneaking into the wards to say goodbye to wives and girlfriends; visiting hours were very strict but she would let them in – many of them, unfortunately, would never come back. Later she was transferred to an old stately home in Oxfordshire; the family owners there had lost their sons in the First World War and had temporarily transformed the building into a nursing home (it is now a police training college). She recalled the uniformed staff standing in the dining room and a large sideboard set out with silver-lidded salvers. It was the first time she had come across kippers for breakfast. It was also where she developed her remarkable map-reading skills – she had to get the ambulances from the East End of London to Oxford at night with no lights and no signposts, the latter having been removed. There was later to be much excitement amongst the nurses as American troops camped on the grounds during the build-up to D-Day. They stayed briefly and were gone silently before dawn one morning. On 6 June 1944, a momentous day in the history books – when the D-Day invasion took place – Eil returned to Ireland in order to tend to her ailing father back home.

As with Cecil Montgomery and Henry Beggs, 14 August was a significant day for John Bernard McCormack of Brosna, County

Kerry, an air gunner on a Blenheim with 23 Squadron at Martlesham Heath. Returning from a night patrol, the Blenheim overturned on landing. The aircraft, beyond being repairable, was written off. He, however, escaped serious injury – as he did for the duration of the Battle of Britain. Unfortunately, this was not so for the duration of the war: in September 1942, while serving with 102 Squadron, operating Halifaxes from Pocklington, his aircraft came down in the North Sea on a raid to Dusseldorf. All crew were lost. He was 23 years old.

Flight Officer Rupert Frederick Smythe was a member of 32 Squadron at Gravesend and born in Killiney, County Dublin. His first 'kill' was over Dunkirk on 2 June 1940, destroying a Junkers 88 – and probably a Messerschmitt 109. On a patrol over France on 11 June he destroyed a Heinkel; on 4 July he destroyed two Messerschmitt 109s. With the intensification of aerial combat after Adlertag, the number of aircraft he took down became more concentrated. On 14 August 1940 he was heavily involved in aerial combat, successfully accounting for a Messerschmitt. Again, over England on 16 August, he destroyed a Dornier 17 'flying pencil' and, on 19 August, he probably downed another Messerschmitt. He did damage to two Dorniers on 20 August and 22 August, respectively. Over Folkestone two days later, however, he was to come out on the wrong side of a tussle with a Messerschmitt 109 and was shot down, crashing at Lyminge. Wounded, he was taken to the Royal Masonic Hospital at Hammersmith. He was awarded the DFC on 30 August 1940 and rejoined 32 Squadron on 1 November, a day after the official end of the Battle of Britain. He did not return to operational flying, but rather took up duties as an instructor and was released from the RAF in 1946.

Dubliner Flight Officer John Allman Hemingway was to be shot down four times during the course of the war. In July 2019, on the occasion of Hemingway's 100th birthday, an interview in *The Irish Times* by Joseph Quinn described his involvement in the Battle of France with 85 Squadron, flying Hurricanes and providing air support for the BEF – and how he had good reason to remember 11 May. On that date he shot down a Dornier 77; later his own aircraft was brought down by anti-aircraft fire over Maastricht and he made a forced landing. He later flew air support sorties over Dunkirk during the evacuation and, while embroiled in the Battle of Britain, the days that followed Adlertag also had reason to stick out in his memory. During that month, he was shot down twice. The first occasion, 18 August, saw him bail out of his Hurricane after it was damaged by returned fire from a Junkers 88 that he engaged over the Thames Estuary; he fell into the sea and had to be rescued from the water, twelve miles east of Clacton. The second incident was on 26 August; he was shot down by a Messerschmitt 109 over Eastchurch and again managed successfully to bail out, his Hurricane crashing into Pitsea marshes, where the local Home Guard picked him up. The site of the Pitsea marshes was excavated in March 2019 and the well-preserved engine, grip joystick and gun button, switched to 'fire', were recovered. On the last day of August, he damaged a Messerschmitt 109. It would be April 1945 before he had to bail out once more, this time from a Spitfire over Italy. Once again, he had defied death; he retired from the RAF in September 1969 as group captain.

After Adlertag it was scramble after scramble. Everything were helter skelter – a madcap effort involving unceasing calls to action. 'The Hardest Day', as it came to be known, was on 18 August; there were almost non-stop incoming raids, the air fighting was ferocious, the engagements were tough, and the casualty count continuously mounting. On this day, Flight Officer Frederick Thomas Gardiner, from Belfast and with 610 Squadron at Gravesend, destroyed a Messerschmitt 110 south-east of Biggin Hill. A week later he was shot down while in combat with Messerschmitt 109s over Dover; he successfully bailed out, only slightly wounded, his Spitfire crashing. He was admitted to Waldershare Hospital.

Impatient for victory, the Luftwaffe was eager for success and increasingly intolerant of resistance. Some fifty attacks on thirteen airfields had to have had its effect on Fighter Command's capability to defend the skies; the use of some of the airfields was denied to them, but only temporarily. Fighter Command's depth of organisation allowed for fighter aircraft to be withdrawn from 11 Group's area when necessary; pilots were then rotated from other groups, allowing some degree of respite for those hard-pressed on the front line of south-east England. This, of course, exposed less experienced pilots to the full fury of combat, some of whom did not survive their involvement – their yet-to-be-perfected dogfighting skills brutally laid bare.

The movement of aircraft to airfields and aerodromes further inland, and the use of locally prepared, temporary airstrips, kept the vital quota of RAF fighter aircraft intact and airborne during this crucial phase of the battle. Fighter aircraft were camouflaged and dispersed, keeping the number of fighter aircraft destroyed on the ground to a minimum – less than sixty in all. Local work parties also played a part, repairing bomb-damaged runways and airstrips. This inbuilt flexibility and adaptability significantly aided the efforts to keep the airfields operational and Fighter Command's fleet in the air. A lot of damage was sustained to airfield buildings at Croydon, Detling, Eastchurch, Hawkinge, Lyminge, Martlesham and West Malling, among others. Some of the airfields were heavily cratered; radar installations had been hit and several aircraft factories had been bombed. In the midst of all this intensity, the men and women of Fighter Command (Irish among them) succeeded in getting their fighter aircraft airborne and offering an effective resistance. It was taking its toll, however, given the number of aircraft lost and, more especially, the shrinking reservoir of pilots. More pilots were being killed than the flight training schools could replace, and those not killed were becoming, if they weren't already, totally exhausted. Fighting fatigue was taking hold and by September 1940 there were eleven pilots from 85 Squadron lost in action and they had to be withdrawn. This was Dubliner John Hemingway's squadron. In *The Irish Times* Hemingway described his commanding officer Peter Townsend (famed for his later romance with Britain's Princess Margaret) as a 'first class wartime leader'. He related how Townsend was good at recognising the signs of battle fatigue – symptoms he saw in John Hemingway. He rested Hemingway with light duties for two years; Hemingway took on a new role as a flight controller, directing fighter air traffic during the Normandy invasion. Keen to get back to flying, he was posted to Italy in September 1944 as leader of 44 Squadron, flying Spitfires.

It was at this stage of the battle, on 20 August, that Prime Minister Winston Churchill delivered a speech in the House of Commons with the famous lines:

> The gratitude of every home in our island, in our Empire and indeed throughout the world, except in the abodes of the guilty, goes out to British airman, who, undaunted by odds, unwearied in their constant challenge and mortal danger, are turning the tide of the world war by their prowess and by their devotion. Never in the field of human conflict was so much owed by so many to so few.

As with 85 Squadron, 65 Squadron was sent to Scotland for a rest. One of their members, Dubliner Brendan 'Paddy' Finucane, was promoted there to flying officer on 3 September. Churchill was to become an admirer of Paddy Finucane, who, as this early course of the war progressed, was to become a fighter ace, much beloved by the media, with an accredited list of some thirty enemy aircraft destroyed. He was to become the youngest ever wing commander on 21 June 1942, leading the Hornchurch Wing. His fiancée, Jean Woolford, lived next door but one. He was to be awarded the DFC in May 1941 – adding two bars to this in September – and a DSO in October. It was a remarkable achievement. He did some of his most noteworthy flying as flight commander of a newly formed unit, which was to become the first Australian squadron in England. It was involved in a number of post-Battle of Britain raids, across the Channel, into northern France; between early August and mid-October 1941 Paddy Finucane claimed at least sixteen enemy fighters, another major achievement – not only in terms of the tally, but, more especially, in the short time it took.

Ironically, and tragically, the demise of so great a pilot was the result of a simple incident: after attacking ships at Ostend and strafing a German airfield on 15 July 1942, the wing reformed to return to Hornchurch. As it passed over the beach at Pointe du Touquet at low level, Finucane's Spitfire was hit by hopeful machine-gun fire from the ground and his radiator was damaged. His engine began to overheat and he prepared to bail out, but he was too low. The engine stopped and, forced to ditch, he crashed into the sea. No trace of him was ever found. He was 21 years old. His last words, heard over the radio before hitting the water, were 'This is it chaps.' Although an Irish citizen, Brendan 'Paddy' Finucane was a national hero in Britain. A requiem mass was held for him in Westminster Cathedral in London and some 3,000 people attended. A nationwide appeal resulted in the bequeathing of the 'Finucane Ward' in Richmond Royal Hospital. Brendan's father Andy had been an active member of the Old IRA, fighting against the Black and Tans during the Irish War of Independence (1919–21); Andy's father, in turn, fought in the British army during the First World War (1914–18).

Winston Churchill was later to say of Brendan Finucane, on 28 October 1948, in a parliamentary debate in the House of Commons:

> I well know the grievous injury which Southern Irish neutrality and the denial of Southern Irish ports inflicted upon us in the recent war, but I always adhered to the policy that nothing, save British existence and survival, should lead us to regain those ports by force of arms because we had already given them up.

> In the end we got through without this step. I rejoice that no new blood was shed between the British and Irish peoples. I shall never forget – none of us can ever forget – the superb gallantry of the scores of thousands of southern Irishmen who fought as volunteers in the British Army and of the famous Victoria Crosses which eight of them gained by their outstanding valour. If ever I feel a bitter feeling rising in my heart about the Irish, the hands of heroes like Finucane seem to stretch out to soothe it away.

Other such southern Irish participants included John Ignatius Kilmartin, born in Dundalk, County Louth. Flying with 43 Squadron at Tangmere, he claimed a Messerschmitt 110 on 6 September 1940 and a Messerschmitt 109 the following day. Previously, during the Battle of France, he had been heavily involved in the fighting; he had an impressive tally, destroying and damaging some fifteen enemy aircraft, overall. This streak was interrupted when his squadron's commanding officer requested a withdrawal to England in late May 1940 due to the state of exhaustion of its pilots.

Rested, he was then posted to Sutton Bridge to instruct at 6 OTU, and later 5 OTU at Aston Down. He crashed on the aerodrome at 6 OTU in mid-August but was unhurt. Early the following month he rejoined 43 Squadron at Tangmere, returning to operational flying and aerial combat; it was a crucial stage of the battle when the supply of pilots was becoming seriously stretched. He survived the battle and the war, remaining in service with the RAF and retiring as wing commander in July 1958, by which time he had been awarded a DFC, in October 1940, and made an OBE, in January 1945.

The Hardest Day, 18 August 1940, saw Belfast-born Frederick Thomas Gardiner flying a Spitfire with 610 Squadron at Gravesend. On 25 July he damaged a Messerschmitt 109 in the Dover/Folkestone area and was himself slightly wounded in the exchange. During the ramped-up aerial exchanges of the Hardest Day, he destroyed a Messerschmitt 110 south-east of Biggin Hill; on 25 August, a week later, he himself was shot down over Dover. He bailed out, slightly wounded, and was admitted to Waldershare Hospital. His Spitfire crashed and burned out on Stoneheap Farm near Northbourne.

Corporal Robertina ('Robina') Nesham, from Sligo, had joined the WAAF along with her two cousins, one of whom was Rosaline McCormick. Nesham drove a three-tonne 'monster' munitions truck and, given her skills in motor mechanics, was well able to keep it roadworthy. She and her cousins were typical of many

Irish women who made a valuable contribution at a vital time, be they in uniform, in the hospitals, or in the munitions and aircraft production factories.

Coping so far, Fighter Command was feeling the weight of the steady force applied by the Luftwaffe. On one day alone, on 31 August, some forty RAF fighters were shot down and fourteen pilots killed. It was Fighter Command's worst day of the battle so far. By this stage the majority of 11 Group's airfields had been attacked and badly damaged. They were still in the fight, but the intensity of the battle was taking its toll. It was struggling to contain the Luftwaffe; the last two days of August highlighted this, seeing some of the Luftwaffe's largest raids and exerting a huge burden upon the RAF. Was this duress bearable? Would the strain become too much? Were they operating on the very fringes, and would it be a matter of days before they were broken? German intelligence certainly believed so. And then something entirely unscripted happened.

IO

PHASE FOUR – GERMAN AIR ATTACKS ON LONDON

Phase Four (7 September–2 October) again saw the Luftwaffe change their objective, this time engaging in large-scale day and night attacks against London – many believe that the encounters during 15 September were the battle's climax.

German intelligence was flawed. 11 Group's airfields, although hit hard, then harder again, were not rendered totally unusable. Most of their fighter strength remained intact. Fighter Command was stretched, but still operational. That it could continue to resist if the current level of pressure from the Luftwaffe was maintained, or increased, was questionable; historians have debated this uncertainty for decades. The common assertion is that it was only days away from being broken, while others suggest that a defence could be mustered indefinitely – that the RAF could repair its airfields, replenish its aircraft and replace its pilots, though the last with more difficulty.

Fighter aircraft losses for the month of August were strangely similar on both sides, the Luftwaffe and RAF sustaining slightly less than 450 fighter aircraft losses each. A similar number of Luftwaffe bomber aircraft were also destroyed, approximately 900 Luftwaffe aircraft losses in total. Despite this, the Luftwaffe commanders may well have believed they had done enough – that 11 Group's resolve was shattering and that their pummelling of airfield targets was paying off. Logically, for them, it was timely to turn their attentions to the next stage of the pre-invasion tactical offensive. Their campaign plan called for the destruction of economic and civic strongholds – industrial, military, transport and other – in order to reduce Britain's capabilities and upset the people's psychological will. With this they hoped to achieve surrender terms, making an invasion unnecessary. But, in case this didn't occur, German troops and equipment continued to be assembled in northern France for the invasion of southern England. The Luftwaffe had been softening up the invasion area. Their attacks concentrated on Fighter Command's 11 Group, hoping to push the RAF northwards, beyond the Thames, so as to grant unimpeded – or at least far less hampered – access onto the shoreline areas selected for landings.

Fighter Command, though badly battered, remained intact; they were still functioning to very good effect. Those involved in round-the-clock shift work, facilitating aircraft production, munitions production and aircraft repair, were also doing their bit to win the battle. And a stock of reserve replacements was always on hand. The biggest problem was in replacing RAF pilots – they were being killed and put out of battle, and the number of trained and experienced replacements to take up the challenge was insufficient. Other than death and injury, there was also the exhaustion that set in with many airmen after exposure to aerial combat. Measures were attempted to address this fatigue: they were made to rest one day in seven, rotated with pilots from other Groups, and moved from airfields at night in order to get a better quality of sleep. Female pilots of the Air Transport Auxiliary were used to ferry aircraft on non-operational missions so as to free up the male pilots for the fighting. The 'Attagirls', as they became known, pioneered female involvement in wartime military aviation; it was yet another manifestation of Britain's pragmatic adaptability, borne out of a spirit of refusal to give in to the demands of Nazi Germany. The mortal danger of Adlertag and the subsequent intensity of the Luftwaffe's aerial assault had not dimmed the marvellous prowess, devotion and effectiveness of Fighter Command.

Then came a surprise. There was neither precedent nor means of preparing for it; it was an unscripted, unimagined happening – arbitrary chance. But its effect suddenly altered the course of events. On the night of 24 August, German bombs fell on residential areas of central London. The accuracy of bombing was not what it is today. It was a mistake, an error – it was even against orders. Whether or not it was believed to be erroneous rather than errant, the following night Wellington bombers, amongst others from Bomber Command, took to the skies over Germany and bombed Berlin. The British bomb raids on Berlin on 25 and 29 August, whether a retaliation for the attack on central London or the ongoing bombing of economic targets, were inconsequential in terms of physical damages, but psychologically they were immeasurable. Outraged, Hitler fumed and vengeance attacks were ordered. The instructions were not without a deadly logic, however. Aerial attacks on London would force Fighter Command into using their fullest strength; the Luftwaffe's intention was to have them become so fully embroiled that they would rid them from the skies. The onslaught against 11 Group's airfields ceased; some historians suggest that it happened just as they were at the point of collapse. Whatever the case, this unexpected turn of events was an opportunity for respite and repair; it was quickly availed of, allowing 11 Group to reorganise and restore themselves to full operational readiness.

The Fuhrer's rhetoric now involved the obliteration of London and a second change of tactics was ordered. London was now to be the Luftwaffe's new point of attack – the primary focus of their fury.

The Luftwaffe penetrating further inland presented Fighter Command with a number of unintended advantages. Not only was 11 Group able to gather its strength, the Luftwaffe were now within easier range of 12 Group and 10 Group, enabling Fighter Command to organise a fuller defence. With London as their destination, the Messerschmitt 109s were operating at the absolute limit of their flight range, meaning their ability to protect German bombers was similarly limited.

As of 7 September, the change in German tactics was unknown to Fighter Command. So when radar detected the slow accumulation of a vast force over the Pas-de-Calais – an aircraft formation almost 1,000 strong – they believed another struggle for the airfields was about to commence. Little did they know that it was the first bid to bomb the English capital.

Squadrons from 10, 11 and 12 Groups took to the skies; they scrambled early and successfully, satisfied that they would intercept the enemy before they reached their objective. But what they thought to be their objective was totally off. They were taken completely by surprise when the enemy air armada headed for London instead, which they reached largely unopposed. Recovering from this surprise, the defenders composed themselves and struck hard as the Germans headed back. The retreating Dornier, Heinkel and Junker bombers and their Messerschmitt escorts were successfully engaged and many were brought down.

Timothy Ashmead Vigors was among those engaged on 7 September, flying a Spitfire and scoring the probable destruction of a Dornier 17 bomber. Vigors had an Anglo-Irish background;

his family were landowners in Ireland for centuries. He had joined 222 Squadron at Duxford in late February 1940 and fought over Dunkirk during the evacuation, securing the probable destruction of a Heinkel on 31 May and a Messerschmitt on 1 June. He successfully shot down a Heinkel III on 19 June, his own Spitfire receiving return fire. On 25 July, with the Battle of Britain firmly under way, Vigors damaged two Heinkel IIIs; on 30 and 31 August he probably destroyed a Messerschmitt 110 and three 109s, but had to make a crash landing at Hornchurch on the second day when his undercarriage failed to come down. Early September was to prove a fruitful period for him. In all he accounted for six enemy aircraft being taken down before he himself was shot down on 9 September, making another crash landing, this time in allotments in Dartford. He was to survive the Battle of Britain and, after many subsequent adventures, the war. He was awarded the DFC in October 1940 and retired from the RAF in November 1946 as a squadron leader, retaining the rank of wing commander. He set up a photographic agency in Ireland, later joining Goffs, the bloodstock auctioneers (horse sales), before starting his own bloodstock agency. After an interlude with a private aviation firm, he again returned to the bloodstock business before inheriting the family farm, Coolmore in County Tipperary, in 1968; he set about building it into a famous stud farm, which he sold in the mid-seventies. He died in 2003.

Oliver Bertram Morrogh-Ryan of Brettanby Manor, Yorkshire, was also involved in the action on 7 September. Born in Meath, he served with 41 Squadron at Hornchurch and on 1 June, over Dunkirk, he shared in the destruction of a Heinkel III. Flying a Spitfire on 5 September, he claimed a Messerschmitt 109; two days later, after combat over Hornchurch, he made a successful forced landing in Great Wakering. He survived the Battle of Britain, but not the war. He was killed whilst conducting searchlight cooperation flying practice in bad weather in July 1941; at the time, he flew a Beaufighter with 68 Squadron at High Ercall. He was 22 years old and is buried in St Cuthbert's Churchyard, Barton, Yorkshire.

Another Spitfire flyer who survived the Battle of Britain but not the war was Kent-born John McAdam, who is buried in Ballyharry Cemetery, Islandmagee, County Antrim. Flying with 41 Squadron at Catterick, he claimed a Dornier destroyed on 7 September. Later the same day, he crashed following combat over Hornchurch at Drake's Farm, Raleigh. His aircraft was partially burned out and was written off; he himself was unhurt. He was again shot down later that month, on 23 September, during a Squadron patrol off Dover. He bailed out and was later rescued from the sea, subsequently being admitted to Dover Hospital. He again crashed at Globe Road, Hornchurch, on 12 October, after his engine cut on take-off. Undaunted, later that month he claimed a Messerschmitt 109. Surviving the Battle of Britain and the various mishaps he was involved in, one would imagine that McAdam had already had his share of ill-fortune, only he was to have one more, with fatal consequences. On 20 February 1941 he was shot down by Major Molders, a Luftwaffe fighter ace, over Dover. He bailed out but was picked up dead from the sea. Vigors, Morrogh-Ryan and McAdam were all involved on 7 September, the opening day of the battle's new phase; a phase that was to see large-scale day and night attacks against London.

It was high summer and German bomber and fighter formations had entered the fray. The Luftwaffe headed for London on 9 and 11 September, but on both occasions Fighter Command intercepted them early on, preventing as many as possible from getting through to the capital. Tearing into the slower-moving bombers, the

Hurricanes did a lot of damage and scattered the formations; the Spitfires engaged the fighter escorts.

'The Greatest Day', on 15 September, has become regarded as the climax of the Battle of Britain. It saw waves of enemy aircraft heading for London and Fighter Command directing separate squadrons to intercept and engage them in aerial ambushes. Some seventeen squadrons were in the skies, poised to resist the incoming enemy formations. The Luftwaffe saw this as the occasion on which they would do away with Fighter Command's resistance once and for all. This was the day in which success in the sky would pave the way for the success of 'Sea Lion', the sea-borne invasion of southern England.

Could those in the RAF do enough to defeat the determined Luftwaffe onslaught? On 15 September, a spectacular shootout between the Luftwaffe and RAF Fighter Command squadrons was vigorously fought. Winning was all important; the consequences of defeat were too dire to imagine.

Determining the outcome were men like Francis Victor Beamish, born in Dunmanway, West Cork; Patrick Joseph Thomas Stephenson, from Dublin; and Anthony Desmond Joseph Carroll Lovell, buried near his home in Portrush Cemetery, County Antrim.

Wing Commander Victor Beamish's father was the headmaster of Dunmanway Model School when Victor was born in September 1903. The family later moved to Coleraine, where Victor attended Coleraine Academical Institution and entered RAF College Cranwell as a flight cadet in 1921; thereafter, he successfully served as a pilot up to 1933, when he had to retire, suffering from tuberculosis. By January 1937, Beamish had sufficiently recovered and was reinstated with full flying status as a flight lieutenant; he was awarded the Air Force Cross (AFC) one year later for establishing the Meteorological Flight (to assist with weather forecasting). He took over RAF North Weald in June 1940, flying operational sorties with his station whenever he could.

Prior to 15 September, Beamish was fully or partly involved in the destruction or damage of some eleven enemy aircraft. On 15 September, again in the thick of the action, flying and fighting to good effect, he had 'a share' in the downing of a Heinkel III. He survived the day's encounters and again put in a skilful and spirited performance on 18 September, 'the hardest fought day'. On 27 September, he probably downed a Messerschmitt 109, going on to damage or destroy four more in the month following, taking him up to the battle's end. He was awarded a DSO in July 1940 and a DFC in November. He was active in many subsequent tussles, but on 28 March 1942 he was involved in an engagement with a Messerschmitt 109 a few miles south of Calais and his aircraft was seen to sustain damage. He was last seen entering clouds near Calais and it was presumed that he crashed into the Channel. He was 38 years old and one of six siblings in the RAF – further to him there were his three brothers, George, Charles and Cecil, and two sisters, Katherine and Eileen. Between them all, the Beamish family provided one air marshal, one air vice marshal, two group captains and two flight lieutenants.

Dublin-born Pilot Officer Patrick Stephenson became so engaged in the air battle on 15 September that his fighter aircraft from 607 Squadron at Usworth collided with a Luftwaffe Dornier 17 bomber over Appledore. He bailed out, slightly wounded by return fire. The Dornier bomber crashed and exploded in the vicinity of Goudhurst. Surviving the battle, he went on to command 607 Squadron in India and Burma, being awarded the DFC in September 1943. Later he was successful against Japanese aircraft until, eventually, he was wounded in combat; he then went on to serve on the personal staff of Lord Louis Mountbatten in Kandy, Ceylon. Appointed wing commander at RAF Fayid, Egypt, he was responsible for converting pilots for service in the Far East. After the war, until 1949, he was assistant air attaché in Paris and was made a companion of the Légion d'Honneur and held the Coeur de Guerre. He resigned from the RAF in July 1955, as squadron leader; he then emigrated to Canada, becoming a citizen in 1960. He died in May 2003.

The initial Luftwaffe aerial onslaught on the morning of 15 September was successfully broken up, only for a bigger force to return in the early afternoon. This too was 'hit up' without hesitation, both on its way to and on its return from London. While bombs did explode in the English capital, they were less intense and more widely dispersed than on the initial surprise attack a week previous. One of those doing the harassing was Anthony Desmond Joseph Lovell, flying a Spitfire with 41 Squadron at Catterick; he was temporary 'B' flight commander. He destroyed a Messerschmitt 109 and probably a second during the day's engagement. He was to go on and destroy or damage four more aircraft before the battle ended on 30 October. He was awarded the DFC in November 1940.

Earlier in the battle, on 28 July, Lovell was attacked by Major Werner Molders, just like John McAdam; he was wounded in the thigh and crash landed at Manston before being admitted to Margate Hospital. Ten days before 'The Greatest Day', on 5 September 1940, he was again shot down; he sustained fire over the Thames Estuary, bailing out unhurt, his Spitfire crashed and burned out in Kimberley Road, South London. The very next day he destroyed a Messerschmitt 109.

Surviving the battle, he went on to command 145 Squadron at Catterick and was awarded a bar to the DFC in February 1942. Further flying exploits and the successful destruction of enemy aircraft saw him awarded the DSO in November 1942, and awarded a bar to the DSO two years later. On 17 August 1945 he crashed a Spitfire into a field adjoining Old Sarum Aerodrome shortly after take-off. He was 26 years old. A year previous, on 29 January 1944, his 27-year-old brother, Flight Lieutenant S.J. Lovell of 183 Squadron, was also killed whilst flying a Typhoon; he was shot down by German anti-aircraft flak.

The significance of 15 September was that it was seen as a turning point in the battle – a turn that favoured Fighter Command. Almost sixty Luftwaffe aircraft were shot down and over double that number of German aircrew were lost; on the side of the RAF, less than thirty fighter aircraft and only thirteen pilots were lost. Fighter Command had regained the initiative, but this alone would not win the battle for them. There was a lot of fighting left to do, but, for now, doubt and disbelief began to pervade the mood of the Luftwaffe; this was especially the case for the Messerschmitt pilots, who had misgivings about the limited combat time they had before having to break off contact over the target area.

Despite this, the outcome of the battle was still very much hanging in the balance. That Fighter Command, and 11 Group especially, had been holding on by a thread after the intense attacks on its airfields is the subject of debate amongst historians. However, what is clear is that, throughout mounting pressure, Fighter Command was able to maintain contact with the enemy without becoming 'decisively engaged', as the Luftwaffe hoped it might. There was still a belief that Hitler's tactic – switching targets from the airfields to day and night attacks on London – might force Fighter Command's hand. The decision, whether it was methodical or emotional, rational or reactive, may well have been a critical misjudgement. Not that this in itself would have turned the tide of the air battle; the German Luftwaffe, intent on raining death and destruction down on London, still had to be deterred. This was the mission of Fighter Command and the end-goal of everyone involved in the war effort. It was a fight, a contest; and losing was not an option.

How this was to be achieved was a matter of constant debate. Vice Air Marshal Leigh-Mallory, of 12 Group, favoured 'Big Wing' tactics; this raised some controversy at the time. At issue was the strength of the attacking squadron sorties. Air Vice Marshal Park, of 11 Group, operated single squadron sorties and occasionally two squadrons together. With responsibility over the south-east, the nearest to northern France, 11 Group were under the greatest pressure, especially of time, and could not overexert themselves by forming up in greater numbers; individual squadrons were also the favoured form of fighting in this war of attrition. Under lesser constraints, Air Vice Marshal Leigh-Mallory took a different approach; he massed his fighters in wing-sized formations – between three and five squadrons – to achieve maximum fire power. The downside to this tactic, argued Air Vice Marshal Park, was that such a concentration of fighters, having formed up and become engaged against the first wave of enemy formations, allowed any succeeding waves through unimpeded. 11 Group had to scramble quickly in order to contest bomber formations and fighter escorts at their fullest strength. Air Vice Marshal Leigh-Mallory's 12 Group engaged the enemy waves after they had already been weakened, so the circumstance favoured the use of concentrated firepower to better inflict losses. In the event, the number of occasions when Big Wing formations engaged enemy bomber formations were few.

With the rate of destruction outweighing the losses sustained, Fighter Command perhaps sensed that the odds were beginning to work in their favour – that the Luftwaffe were to be refused air supremacy. In short, they began to feel that they might be about to win the battle. However, this depended on maintaining the rate of attrition achieved over the last number of days. 18 September was another golden opportunity to do so. The fight for the skies was going their way; this emerging sense of self-belief was empowering and vital.

Flight Lieutenant William Riley was a flight commander with 302 Squadron at Leconfield in September 1940; he was from Manorhamilton, County Leitrim. He was airborne and fighting on 18 September and destroyed a Junkers 88 and probably a second one. On 16 July 1942 he was killed; he was 25 years old. While acting as wing commander with 272 Squadron, his Beaufighter collided with another Beaufighter soon after taking off at Malta on a sortie to intercept a Junkers 52. In October 1941 he had been awarded the DFC.

Wing Commander Victor Beamish was also in action on 18 September and downed a Messerschmitt 109. Beamish was one of four brothers who served in the RAF. The same was the case for Sergeant Peter O'Byrne, born in Coventry in August 1917. On 27 September, flying a Hurricane and in combat with Messerschmitt 110s, he suffered engine damage and had to make a wheels-up landing in Staffhurst Wood, Limpsfield, tearing his wings off in the process. Just prior to the official end of the Battle of Britain in late October, O'Byrne made a crash landing near Leatherhead whilst on a routine patrol in a Hurricane – he was unhurt. He later saw service in the Middle East and India, and, surviving the war, was released from the RAF in 1946 as a warrant officer. His brother

Sergeant Thomas Patrick O'Byrne had been killed in action with 217 Squadron of Coastal Command on 1 February 1941. Peter O'Byrne joined Aer Lingus as a pilot, later flying with Jersey Airlines as a captain until his retirement. He died in June 1998.

On 17 September, with no signs of the Luftwaffe securing air supremacy over the English coast, Hitler decided to postpone Operation Sea Lion indefinitely. Fighter Command, unaware of this, continued its defence of the British airspace, as the threat from the Luftwaffe's bombing formations had yet to wane. The Battle of Britain was far from over.

On 11 September 1940 Alexander William Valentine Green, from Craigavad, County Down, along with his Blenheim crew, fell victim to Messerschmitt 109s who were protecting a convoy off the coast of Calais; the convoy was being attacked by Albacores (bombers) of 826 Naval Air Squadron and Green's crew were acting as the bombers' escort. The Blenheim was shot down into the Channel and all three crew were lost. Green was 21 years old.

Sergeant Matthew Cameron, from Ballinrees, near Coleraine, served with 66 Squadron at Duxford. On 27 September 1940 he claimed the destruction of a Junkers 88, adding to his tally of a Messerschmitt 109 on 20 August; later, fourteen days after the official end of the Battle of Britain, he claimed a Junkers 87. Commissioned in March 1941, he later flew Typhoons, was attached to an air-sea rescue unit, and was a flight commander at 12 Air Gunnery School in Bishops Court, County Down. He survived the war and was released from the RAF in 1945.

During a practice dogfight on 30 September 1940, Sergeant Henry Reginald Clarke, Belfast, was flying a Spitfire with 610 Squadron at Acklington when his fighter aircraft collided head on with another Spitfire. It is likely that Clarke's propeller struck the other aircraft's wing. He successfully bailed out, but fell unconscious; when he came to, he found himself hanging upside down, suspended by one strap that was fastened very insecurely around one leg. He got hold of the rest of the harness after managing to get himself upright, but passed out again just before reaching the ground. He could not remember opening the ripcord of his parachute. Clarke's was an incredible escape; his only injuries were some bruises and a deep cut on the chin. The other Spitfire, flown by Flight Officer C.H. Bacon, crashed on Alnmouth Beach and he was killed. Wreckage from Clarke's aircraft was dug up in 1995 for display in Bamburgh Museum. Clarke went on to fly Defiants and Beaufighters, was commissioned in August 1941, and acted as a test pilot until he was released from the RAF in 1947. He died in July 2010.

Dublin-born Robert Sidney James Edwards was shot down on 30 September while in combat with Dornier 17s and Messerschmitt 110s over Portland. He flew a Hurricane and bailed out. A member of 56 Squadron at Boscombe Down, he was in fact its 'B' Flight Commander. He had only returned to operations three weeks prior, having been shot down while serving with 79 Squadron, a victim of return fire from Heinkel 111s north-west of Mons on 11 May 1940. He bailed out of the Hurricane with burns to one arm. The squadron returned to Biggin Hill, from France, on 20 May. On 18 May, while his arm healed, Edwards was posted to join the admin staff at 11 Group headquarters; he remained there until his return to operational flying in September. He survived the Battle of Britain, moving to Bomber Command, and was awarded the DFC on 21 November 1941, serving with 9 Squadron at Honington. Edwards retired from the RAF on 12 February 1963 as a wing commander. He died in May 1974.

Jerry Hurley was born near Bantry in 1919, and emigrated to Dagenham in east London sometime around 1940. He lived with his sister, Peg Hinchin – her husband, Paddy was from Macroom – in a part of Dagenham that was known colloquially as 'Little Cork' because of all the people from Cork who went to work in Ford's Motor Factory. Ford's had switched car production to building B-24 bombers, jeeps, tank engines, Bren gun carriers and a wide array of other military hardware.

Dagenham became a prime target for German bombers and one night Jerry Hurley was returning to his sister's house in the pitch darkness after an eight-hour shift on the Ford's assembly line, but when he got there, the house had been practically obliterated by a bomb. However, his sister and her family were safe as every street was equipped with bomb shelters where people sought safety when the air raid sirens sounded. Nightly bombing was to become a normal part of life for Jerry and all the other Irish living in Dagenham. Normal too was food rationing; it had been introduced in January 1940; bacon, butter, sugar, meat, tea, jam, biscuits, breakfast cereals, cheese, eggs, lard, milk and canned and dried fruit were all rationed. Fresh vegetables and fruit were not rationed but supplies were limited. Like every adult Jerry Hurley was given a ration book allowing him to buy 57 grams (2 ounces) of butter, 57 grams of cheese and 227 grams of minced meat – equivalent to two lamb chops – each week. After his sister's home was bombed, he lived in lodgings and became very suspicious about the quality of meat the landlady was serving. He made enquiries and found out that it was rat that had been cooked. He immediately spewed it up and switched his digs.

Another story concerned Matron Kathleen Rogers nee Connolly from Co Down who was supervising a ward in a wooden Nissen hut on the grounds of a London hospital during a bombing raid when part of an incendiary bomb came through the skylight in the hut's roof and began burning fiercely on the floor. A young inexperienced orderly, innocently thinking he was doing the right thing, lost no time in picking up the water-filled fire bucket and making a dash down the hut to dose the fire. However, standing between him and the fire, knowing that the throwing of water on the burning incendiary device, would in fact spread not smother the flames, picked up a shovel and smartly smacked the orderly on the head as he passed her, knocking him out cold, and then, with sand, she outed the fire.

Death, victory and close escapes. This was the reality within the complex contest that was the Battle of Britain; and while the tide may have begun to turn in favour of Fighter Command, Reichsmarschall Hermann Goering was not admitting defeat just yet.

II
PHASE FIVE – FIGHTER FIGHT

Phase Five (3 October–31 October) saw the Luftwaffe make yet another tactical change. They now favoured the use of customised fighter aircraft as fighter bombers and undertook small-scale daylight raids with large-scale nightly attacks, mainly against London. This was the start of what came to be known as 'the Blitz' on the capital and other small cities and towns; this continued on after the Battle of Britain, lasting until May 1941.

'Get in fast, hit hard, and get out' was the RAF fighter pilot's adage. Over the course of the battle fought thus far, many German aircraft had fallen to RAF fighter attacks. The pace of the exchanges had, first incrementally, then rapidly, picked up and the cumulative losses of German bombers had seriously weakened the Luftwaffe. German fighter aircraft were outmanoeuvred, often left confused during aerial skirmishing. Protracted dog fights were a rarity. The speed of the aerial combat; the dives, rolls and inverted flight; the attacks out of the sun and retreats into the clouds; the short, sharp staccato bursts of cannon and machine-gun fire, instantaneous, then over. It was a great strain for anyone in the cockpit to keep up. The rate of attrition inflicted on the Luftwaffe meant their offensive power was rapidly dwindling. The daylight bombing sorties above the larger English cities, and London in particular, were costing the Germans dearly in terms of aircraft and aircrew. Fighter Command were also losing fighter aircraft and pilots, but in far fewer numbers. And the degree of RAF losses was offset by fighter aircraft production and repairs. It was time for the Luftwaffe to reconsider their schedule of large-scale daylight raids. So began the next phase of the battle: small-scale daylight fighter-bomber attacks followed by large-scale night attacks, mainly against London. Some historians consider this as the commencement of what came to be referred to as 'the Blitz', which lasted into the middle of the following year, 1941.

'Jabo', short for 'Jagdbomber' (fighter bomber), were Messerschmitt 109s fitted with a modified underfuselage that held a single 250kg bomb; they were sent individually or in groups to bomb English cities by day. If intercepted en route, they could jettison their bomb in advance of arriving at their target, engaging their attackers or attempting to evade their attentions. The attached single bomb made the aircraft slower and less manoeuvrable; despite this, many got through and delivered their deadly load. This further change of tactics was ordered by the head of the Luftwaffe, Hermann Goering, who was more positive than his pilots that this new initiative might bring about a rapid resolution to the battle – a result that, so far, had proved frustratingly elusive. Up to now, small squadrons of well-placed Spitfires and Hurricanes, using surprise, speed and height, were successful in penetrating the large, unwieldly Luftwaffe bomber formations; they got in close, lined up the Heinkels, Dorniers and Junker bombers in the crosshairs of their gyro gunsights, and then, with thumbs pressed firmly on the firing buttons, unleashed their eight Browning guns on the target. Now, far faster, more manoeuvrable fighter bombers, with covering escorts, took to the skies in waves – their destination, London.

Fighter Command tactics also changed, with 'standing patrols' already airborne at higher altitudes, waiting for their prey to arrive. Introduced on 15 September, these now included the Spitfire Mark II. The Messerschmitt 109s, slower than usual due to the weight of the attached 250kg undercarriage bomb, were highly susceptible to the Spitfires and Hurricanes which moved at double their speed – losses were high. What's more, the RAF fighter pilots allowed the Luftwaffe fighter bombers to proceed deep into English airspace, where time and distance ensured they had less fuel for the fight. The RAF had more – plenty more – and so were far less constrained during aerial combat.

Dogfights did occur, however. One of the most extraordinary dogfights, on 7 October, involved Kenneth William Mackenzie from Belfast, who flew with 43 Squadron at Usworth. Having already destroyed a Messerschmitt 109, he shared in the downing of a second, only it appeared somewhat inconclusive; following it down to almost sea level, Mackenzie noticed it did not ditch into the water. With no ammunition left, he was unable to issue the final destructive volley; instead, he struck the Messerschmitt 109's tailplane with the wing of his own Hurricane, causing the enemy fighter to crash into the sea. Mackenzie then had to make a forced landing at Hope Farm near Folkestone, suffering slight facial injuries. On 25 October he claimed the destruction of a Messerschmitt 109, shared in the destruction of another, and yet another damaged. Not that this was the end of the day's drama. On a later patrol he collided with Pilot Officer Vilém Goth of 501 Squadron as he manoeuvred his section to attack a formation of Messerschmitt 109s. Mackenzie bailed out unhurt, but Goth was killed when he crashed in Bridgehurst Wood, Marden. Mackenzie was later awarded the DFC in October 1940, going on to destroy three further Messerschmitts before the month ended.

Kenneth William Mackenzie survived the Battle of Britain and continued to down enemy aircraft until he himself was downed in late September 1941; his aircraft was struck by heavy flak from ground defences while leading a strafing attack on Lannion airfield in Brittany. He ditched into the sea, took to his dinghy and paddled to shore, but was captured and became a prisoner of war (POW). Mackenzie did not like being a POW and became a persistent escapee. He made his first attempt on his way to the POW camp, giving his guard the slip at a crowded Paris railway station only to be swiftly recaptured. He was a determined tunnel-digger at Oflag VI-B, Warburg, Northern Germany, but was fortunate not to have been buried alive when a tunnel collapsed on him; he managed, however, to scramble clear. Undaunted, the tunnelling attempts later continued and on the successful completion of one such tunnel, as the first prisoner crawl from the tunnel exit, he was spotted. Another attempt saw him and a colleague make their way unseen to the camp's perimeter fence; hiding under blankets, they waited for nightfall, when they planned to dig a shallow tunnel under the wire. However, a guard became curious and, while a diversion was created, the two men retreated into the prison compound. A number of weeks later, he was transferred to Stalag Luft III at Sagan, where, over a long period of time, he feigned madness, developing a severe stammer as part of the act. He was repatriated in October 1944 and took up duties as an instructor. Surviving the war, he remained in the RAF, seeing service in Kenya and Zambia. He retired from the RAF, as a wing commander, in 1967, having been awarded the AFC in 1953. He then became deputy commander of the newly independent Zambian Air Force until 1970; thereafter, he was managing director of Air Kenya in Nairobi for three years, at which point he retired. He then moved to Cyprus before returning to the UK in 2000. He died in 2009; he was 92 years old.

The combat performance of the Spitfires and Hurricanes was developed over time; their development involved tests – these tests involved test flights. Norman Lancelot Ievers, born in Patrickswell, County Limerick, later moving to Bray, County Wicklow, and then Belfast, was, eventually, to become a test pilot. But first he was posted to 312 Squadron at Speke, composed of Czechoslovakian pilots and English commanders; here, he operated Hurricanes. Their role was to intercept Luftwaffe bombers attacking Liverpool. He flew many operational patrol sorties during his time, but no contact with the enemy was made. In late November 1940, post-Battle of Britain, he reported to the newly formed High Altitude Flight at the Aeroplane and Armament Experimental Establishment, Boscombe Down. His testing career mostly involved experiments – experiments that would eventually lead to the introduction of pressurised cockpits. These tests involved flying at altitudes up to and in excess of 40,000 feet, and, on one occasion, involved an engine failure followed by a forced landing.

Ievers returned to Fighter Command in July 1941, joining with 257 Squadron, whose role was to protect convoys over the North Sea. Afterwards, he commanded 80 Squadron in North Africa, which was very active, operationally. A short spell on the air staff in Cairo was followed by a Rangoon-bound posting. However, on his way there the city fell to the Japanese and so the ship he was travelling on docked at Colombo, Ceylon (now Sri Lanka), whereupon he was sent to Calcutta, India, to test-fly assembled parts shipped out from England; on one occasion, when the aircraft was assembled with the controls reversed, he was almost victim to a fatal crash. He survived the war, being released from the RAF in 1944, and he returned to Ireland, eventually settling at Mount Ievers, County Clare. He died in November 1993. His eldest brother also served in the RAF but was killed in a road accident in 1939.

Dublin-born Frederick Joseph Aldridge of 41 Squadron, flying a Spitfire, had a bountiful period towards the end of this phase of the battle. During aerial combat on 17, 25 and 30 October, he claimed three Messerschmitt 109s, destroyed or damaged. 30 October was the eve of the battle's very last 'official' day. Pilot Officer Aldridge survived the battle and shortly thereafter was assigned to 308 Polish Fighter Squadron, Baginton. The Polish played a significant part in the Battle of Britain, with a noticeably high kill rate; the highest of any RAF squadron during the battle. A worthy involvement, not always fully recognised. Before his release from the RAF in 1947, Aldridge served in a variety of overseas postings, including Palestine, Libya and Canada.

Mid-October 1940 saw Sergeant Ernest Henry Clarke Kee's Hurricane severely damaged in combat, causing it to crash at Dunton Green. Kee escaped without injury. From Ballybofey, County Donegal, he was posted to 253 Squadron at Kirton in Lindsey in early June, flying with them throughout the duration of the battle, which, despite a near-death misadventure on 15 October, he survived. He did not, however, survive the war. On 20 April 1944, as an acting squadron leader with 241 Squadron – a reconnaissance unit in the coastal area of Šibenik–Zadar (Croatia) – his aircraft was hit by anti-aircraft fire from two heavily defended schooners while he went on a strafing run. He was awarded the DFC in December 1945, back-dated to the day before his death.

Sergeant John Keatinge Haire, from Belfast, flying a Hurricane with 145 Squadron, had a part share in the probable destruction of a Junkers 88 on 23 October. He survived the Battle of Britain, only to die six days later, at 20 years of age, when his Hurricane sustained damage. It was burning fiercely from combat over the Isle of Wight, but he opted to remain with his aircraft until the last possible moment to ensure it did not crash into the small village below; only after it had been cleared did he jump. However, he miscalculated, leaving it too late and his parachute did not have time to deploy properly.

Thomas Andrew McCann, from County Down, also flew a Hurricane. From mid-September until the battle's end, he flew with 601 Squadron at Exeter; he was then posted to 134 Squadron, who operated in tandem with 81 Squadron, forming 151 Wing. They fought in Russia, making use of Vaenga Airfield near Murmansk. Their operations included bomber escorts and, in mid-November 1941, pilots of 134 Squadron began converting Russian pilots on to Hurricanes; they departed later that month, leaving all their equipment with them. McCann was killed on 27 July when, south-west of Alexandria, Egypt, his squadron, scrambling from Landing Ground 154, was 'bounced' by Messerschmitt 109s as they took off. McCann was 23 years old and is buried in El Alamein War Cemetery.

The battle's fifth and final phase was coming to an end. The air supremacy required to bring Operation Sea Lion into effect remained a distant prospect for the Luftwaffe It was at this stage of the battle's proceedings that the Corpo Aereo Italiano – the Italian Air Expeditionary Force – entered the fray and, on 24 October, made their first sudden attack in an evening raid on Harwich. Mussolini had previously declared the intention that his air force was to support the Luftwaffe and so bask in the reflective glory of victory over the RAF. By the time they managed to assist, however, the battle was almost at an end; the Italians dropped bombs on Britain, albeit very few and very badly. They would have gone on doing so, only they were unequivocally stopped by the RAF, paying a heavy price in an unequal fight. In outdated Fiat BR.20 bombers, escorted by Fiat G.50 and CR.42 bi-plane fighters, a large formation targeted Ramsgate Harbour, in daylight on 29 October. En route, they were intercepted by anti-aircraft fire, prematurely dropped their bombs on Deal instead, and promptly returned to their airfields in Belgium. It was to be eleven days after the official end of the Battle of Britain before the Italian bombers and bi-planes encountered the RAF in an aerial encounter. It took place over the Thames Estuary and, when faced up against RAF Hurricanes, the outcome was inevitable: there were losses on the Italian side, none on the RAF's.

So there was neither victory nor glory for the Italians to have a share in. The crucial period of combat had ended, and, without guaranteed air cover, the Luftwaffe's hoped-for invasion was not militarily viable. The Luftwaffe had not succeeded in its aim; Fighter Command had. Hitler turned his attentions towards Russia and the Eastern Front. The Battle of Britain was over, Fighter Command had won, and men and women from Ireland had contributed to its success.

12

AFTER THE BATTLE

The Luftwaffe was prepared for a short Blitzkrieg-type campaign, securing air superiority over England in advance of Operation Sea Lion – a swift invasion of the poorly protected beaches of southern England. They did not succeed in coaxing Fighter Command to fight under circumstances that favoured them, allowing them the opportunity to deploy their numerical advantage to good effect. Initially overconfident, their impressive front-line strength – 2,800 aircraft – was worn down by attrition as they suffered continued losses from the very beginning. Flying over the Channel stretched the range of their bomber formations' fighter escorts; their sorties were further exacerbated by hard-hitting squadrons of Spitfires and Hurricanes. The RAF's interceptions were guided by radar, which was carefully integrated with Observer Corps watchers and the Dowding system; the Luftwaffe, for their part, completely underestimated the momentous advantage of this integration.

Compounding this situation, German intelligence was inaccurate; they overestimated Fighter Command's losses, so the collapse they forecasted never actually materialised. With the Luftwaffe's losses mounting, adequate reserves lacking, and favourable conditions – weather, tides and time – passing, Reichsmarschall Hermann

Goering diverted his bombers onto RAF airfields, particularly 11 Group's, which were scattered across Kent and Sussex. In turn, a subsequent decision by Hitler, perhaps premature, again changed the Luftwaffe's point of attack, this time placing the focus on English cities, but London especially. But while German aircraft blackened the skies over southern England, their pilots' morale declined in the face of an RAF fighter force which, contrary to what they had been told, was far from dwindling.

Within an hour of take-off, the Luftwaffe fighter pilots had to turn back and return to bases in northern France and Belgium. If not, a shortage of fuel threatened forced landing or the need to bail out and ditch their Messerschmitt 109s into the Channel, which many of them did. For the German bomber and fighter pilots, the Battle of Britain was totally different to the previous campaigns of the war. The fighter pilots, particularly, were restricted in their role as bomber escorts, having to fly in close proximity to bomber formations at slow speeds. This became a major cause of casualties to both bomber and fighter crews.

Cleverly treating it as a battle of attrition, Fighter Command's conduct during the Battle of Britain proved decisively correct. By holding their nerve, their resolve never wavered. And despite the sturdy framework they had prepared, Fighter Command were not averse to making technical and technical adaptions when necessary. They 'widened out' the Vic formation, allowing all fighter pilots, not just the formation leader, to keep an eye out for the enemy and to search the skies more freely. Their pilots flew 'standing patrols' in order to provide early warning and direct, at even shorter notice, an attack that would disperse the Luftwaffe bombers. The Spitfire was modified: its engine's fuel system was adjusted to fuel injection instead of float-type carburettor; the propellers were changed to total variable pitch; the engine was updated to Merlin III Rolls-Royce; and they began to use 'De Wilde' ammunition, an incendiary type round. Hard experiences resulting in lessons learned. Using tactics, technology and teamwork, Fighter Command proved a formidable force; they fought a clever battle with a measured intensity, denying the Luftwaffe their objective.

With invasion looming and freedom at stake – and Churchill famously unwilling to seek terms from Hitler – a successful defence was a necessity. Significantly, the battle's successful outcome was critically important in contributing to the later winning of the war. It was one of the war's crucial turning points, and it was facilitated by the individual ability of the RAF pilots (Irishmen amongst them), the Dowding system, and the combat performance of the Hurricane and the Spitfire. Had the Battle of Britain ended differently, with the Luftwaffe securing air superiority and the Wehrmacht gaining unhindered passage across the Channel from occupied France and Belgium, then Hitler, with all of Europe under the Nazi jackboot, would have been able to concentrate his forces against Russia. With only the Eastern Front to focus on, he wouldn't have had to disperse his military assets, and would have had a far greater chance of defeating the Soviets.

The landmass provided by Britain and Northern Ireland was crucial during Allied preparations for D-Day – the opening of the 'Second Front' – making it logistically feasible; without such a platform, there may well have been no American intervention. It was from a secure Britain that Bomber Command and the US Airforce conducted its bombing campaigns, both before and after the D-Day invasion on 6 June 1944.

There was an air offensive, after D-Day, aimed at damaging the Nazi regime's military industrial complex in the Ruhr, softening up German resistance so that Allied ground troops could eventually seize and hold enemy territory in Continental Europe. This advance also included the destruction of Hitler's 'secret weapons' and the launch sites of the Vergeltungswaffen (Vengeance Weapons), the V-1 and V-2.

The Battle of Britain, described by many as the greatest air battle in the history of warfare, saw air power come of age. Land force commanders could not, after this point, move their forces without being sure of air cover; the air was now a vital factor affecting the outcome of operations. It is important to remember, however, that the Battle of Britain wasn't won by Fighter Command alone; victory also relied on the efforts of Anti-Aircraft Command, Coastal Command, Bomber Command, the Observer Corps, Civil Defence, the Royal Navy and the aircraft and munitions factory workforces. The combined efforts of all, manifested in the capabilities of those who fought in the air, determined the battle's outcome.

Combat saw machines pitted against each other: fighter aircraft versus fighter aircraft. Skirmishes were akin to aerial jousting matches, involving aggressive manoeuvring and shots at the jugular; great speeds, heights and aerial acrobatics were needed to prevail. The ongoing aerial exchanges, had, from the Luftwaffe's point of view, seen the RAF brought close to defeat at the height of the battle – but that this victory was spoiled by Hitler's interference. A moment of jubilance turned to jeopardy.

Although there is an 'official' timeline for the battle's duration – between 10 July and 31 October – entitling aircrew involved to be awarded the Battle of Britain clasp, there is a valid belief, held by many, that the Battle of Britain could be considered to have begun as soon as the Battle of France ceased, and that it continued on, into the Blitz, until May 1941. Whatever the case, the action that took place from mid-July until the end of October makes for a compelling history, many of whose surviving participants went on to have other exhilarating involvements, both before and after the war ended.

One such participant was Harold John Maguire, born in Kilkishen, County Clare, and educated at Wesley College and Trinity College Dublin. Joining the RAF on a short service commission, he began flight training in March 1933; later he joined 230 Flying Boat Squadron at Pembroke Dock, serving with it in Egypt and the Far East. In March 1939, Maguire, back in the UK, was granted a medium service commission and, in October 1939, was in command of 229 Squadron at Digby. On 28 May 1940, over Dunkirk, he damaged a Dornier 17. Afterwards, in early September 1940, he was posted to 6 Operational Training Unit, Sutton Bridge, as squadron leader.

The Battle of Britain and the Blitz over, in late 1941 he was posted to Singapore as wing commander, flying with the proposed 266 Wing. After the fall of Singapore, the RAF evacuated to Sumatra, but the speed of the Japanese advance meant it fell to him to organise the defence of P1 Airfield at Palembang against the Japanese paratroopers. In mid-February 1942, after having led seven Hurricanes to P1, they found it under heavy attack from Japanese fighter aircraft. Maguire claimed a Zero (a Japanese fighter aircraft) before landing. The airfield was cut off once surrounded by the Japanese and he took charge of its ground defence. Supplementing armaments, they stripped their aircraft of the Browning machine guns and lowered the Bofors anti-aircraft guns to give a horizontal instead of vertical line of fire. With twenty men, little ammunition, and barely enough food and water, taking on the advancing Japanese was not a promising prospect.

They took up position in a slit trench and several Japanese were similarly dug in; but when the Japanese broke cover and became unexpectedly exposed, Maguire and a fellow officer opened fire and killed a number of them. When the attackers were reinforced, the situation worsened and Maguire, remembering the army adage 'when in doubt, proceed with full confidence', strode forward. He demanded to meet their commanding officer and then informed him that the Japanese were vastly outnumbered, advising him to surrender. This desired result did not materialise, but safe passage was negotiated and, on the pretext of consulting a non-existent superior officer, Maguire returned to the airfield and organised the destruction of all aircraft and equipment. It took a week to trek to the west coast of Sumatra, where a coaster brought them to Batavia. The Japanese advance proved unstoppable and, giving up his place on one of the last aircraft leaving Java to a wounded pilot, he was subsequently taken prisoner. Inmates at Boci Gledale POW camp experienced conditions of great hardship, but Maguire stood up to the bullying treatment of the Japanese, exhibiting great care for those under his command. With the arrival of peace, he compiled a dossier on the war crimes perpetrated by his captors, put the 'bad time' behind him, and resumed his career in Fighter Command. He was made officer in charge at Linton-on-Ouse, flying the twin piston-engined de Havilland Hornet. From 1950–52 he commanded RAF Odiham in Hampshire, where a wing of the de Havilland Vampire Jets was located. In 1955 he moved to Malta as senior air staff officer, returning to the Air Ministry the next year to direct tactical and air transport operations.

Still flying, now as air marshal, in 1959, Maguire displayed great presence of mind when his engine failed ten minutes after flying over Whitehall in a display commemorating the Battle of Britain.

He picked out a cricket pitch and successfully landed on the square, breaking the stumps at one end, while the teams were off having tea. When he entered the pavilion, nursing an injured back, he was welcomed by the players with a strong cup of Darjeeling tea.

He returned to the Far East in 1962 to take part in the Indonesian confrontation; he began as a senior air staff officer, next becoming assistant chief of air staff (intelligence) and, in 1965, deputy chief of defence staff (intelligence). Three years later he retired from the RAF as an air marshal, but was recalled to become the Ministry of Defence's director general of intelligence for four more years. From the mid-1940s to the early 1980s, he was director of an insurance group (Commercial Union) and its political and economic advisor. After his final retirement, Maguire remained active in the area in which he lived, Brantham, Suffolk; he was chairman of the local Conservative Association and the local branch of the British Legion. He was also a keen member of the Royal Harwich Yacht Club. During the course of his career, he received three mentions in despatches, in 1940, 1942 and 1946. He was awarded the DSO in October 1946 and was made an OBE in January 1950, a CB in 1958 and was created KCB in 1966. He died in 2001.

An article in *The Irish Press* on 2 May 1949 was to tell another story of the varying post-war fates in store for RAF wartime participants. It concerned an ex-RAF officer found dead at Walton Lodge, Caragh Lake, County Kerry. Captain David John North-Bomford, a native of County Meath, was found lying dead outside the front door of his house at about 10 p.m. with a shotgun between his legs. Originally joining the RAF on a short service commission in 1934, he subsequently joined III Squadron at Northolt. After joining the staff of the Electrical and Wireless School at Cranwell, he was posted to RAF Hinaidi, Iraq with 53 Squadron. He resigned his commission in April 1937, joining the RAFVR in January 1939 as an airman u/t pilot. Called up on 1 September, he completed training and served with 229 Squadron from early 1940. He moved to 17 Squadron at Debden in late July 1940 and became attached, briefly, to 601 Squadron on 25 August, flying some sorties with them before being attached to III Squadron, also at Debden, and moving back to 17 Squadron from 17 September. In mid-October he was posted to 7 Operational Training Unit Hawarden as a flying instructor. He was released from the RAF in 1947 and took his own life on 28 April 1949.

The article in *The Irish Press*, entitled 'Died from Gun Shot Wound in Mouth', described the verdict at the inquest of 36-year-old Captain David J. North-Bomford, ex-British Air Force. David John's father, reportedly said that his son had taken part in some hectic engagements during the Battle of Britain – that he had also seen service in other theatres and that he had a few very 'close shaves'. He had noticed that, as a result of these activities, his son was suffering from nervous tension which at times appeared to become acute. Mrs Bomford, his widow, reportedly said that her husband and herself were in Cork that day and had returned only about an hour before the tragedy occurred. She had also noticed that David, at times, appeared to suffer from nervous tension. He was inclined to become impatient about little things. Sympathy was tendered to the relatives. David John North-Bomford was buried at All Saints Church of Ireland churchyard, Moyglare, County Kildare.

There were others who carried physical scars – burns and wounds – long into the war's aftermath, if not all their lives. These injuries and disfigurements are a reminder of the service given and the sacrifice made for freedom – a privilege enjoyed long after the battle.

13

TELLING THE BATTLE OF BRITAIN STORY

Of the 2,938 RAF aircrew that fought in the Battle of Britain, almost half – 1,339 – did not live to see the final victory at the war's end. In June 1940 there seemed to be little or no chance that Britain could withstand the ever-expanding, tyrannical forces of Nazi fascism and Hitler's extreme right-wing dictatorship. Britain's very existence and the continued freedom of its people depended on the outcome of the battle. The Battle of Britain was the story of a struggle for survival. For this reason alone, victory was vitally important – but it was also vital to the course of the war, and the course of history. Britain was strategically important, because it was to act as both a bomber base for offensives into Germany, and, later in the war, as a springboard for the Allied invasion of Nazi-occupied Normandy on D-Day, 6 June 1944.

The Blitz was to follow the Battle of Britain. Indeed, it had begun while the battle was still under way. It was to cause massive destruction around British cities: 40,000 civilian deaths, huge hardship, heartbreak and fear. Many Irish people living and working in England were caught up in the chaos and suffered accordingly. Newly ordained priest Father Charlie Lynch from Cork was among them. His vocational responsibilities involved his attendance at many horrific scenes, where he often gave blood for immediate transfusion to very seriously injured victims. He took cover under ambulances, the bombings sometimes still in progress. These were scenes he never related or spoke of in later life – typical of the many who experienced such tragedy and trauma. The Blitz ended in May 1941. During that summer, Hitler invaded Russia; after the Japanese attack on Pearl Harbor at year's end, the US entered the war.

There are many compelling accounts of those who experienced the Battle of Britain. There is the exhilarating and moving 2006 memoir by Irishman Tim Vigors DFC, *Life's Too Short to Cry*; Doug Stokes' *Wings Aflame* (1985), a biography of Group Captain Victor Beamish DSO and bar, DFC, AFC, and *Paddy Finucane: Fighter Ace* (1983) are similarly convincing in their realism and interesting in their detail. They account for the lives of three among the many Irish participants whose involvement was distinguished by records of courage, determination and selfless sacrifice – whose exceptional engagements ought to be a better known source of pride in their own country.

The battle and those who fought in it have also been commemorated in film. Guy Hamilton's *Battle of Britain* (1969), produced by Harry Saltzman and Benjamin Fisz and based on the book *The Narrow Margin* by Derek Wood and Derek Dempster, was an expensive production with a gallery of famous film stars and spectacular flying sequences. A large number of fighter aircraft from the period were required and sourced, but only a portion were available – fewer still were in flying order. A working fleet of Luftwaffe and RAF aircraft – and five Irish Air Corps TR9 Spitfires (only two of them airworthy) – were used, along with model aircraft, in the filming of realistic aerial combat footage. The two two-seater

TR9 Spitfires housed a camera in the rear seat, which made them ideal. The film contributed, along with exhibitions in museums and further book publications, in relating the story of the Battle of Britain for succeeding decades.

However, serious concerns arose that there was a lack of understanding and appreciation of the battle in 1995, which led Bill Bond MBE to establish the Battle of Britain Historical Society and to take measures to perpetuate the memory of the battle as a pivotal part of history.

Ironically, the historical society initially attracted those who already knew of it, even some who participated in it, but not those who were uninformed. An initiative arose for the creation and construction of 'The Monument to the Few' and a central London site was successfully sourced on Victoria Embankment from the City of Westminster Council. On it was a large, grey stone structure, eighty-two feet long, a disused chimney/smoke outlet for the now-redundant underground steam engines. It was acknowledged by all concerned that it was important to realise the full potential of the site offered. An open competition was held in which artists, designers and sculptors were invited to submit their ideas and concepts. A shortlist of five was selected by the historical society, from which sculptor Paul Day's design emerged as outright winner. Massive bronze panels, huge two-tonne castings of reliefs depicting the spirit of that moment in time, incorporated scenes from the battle as well as the names of the participants. Paul Day understood the national importance of the monument as a fitting tribute and an educational tool, presenting a broad, inclusive vision of the battle, both inside and outside Fighter Command. He wished to make a contemporary work which spoke to post-modernism – which spoke of the now – but resurrected the drama, memory and atmosphere of the Battle of Britain. Working with clay, his was a clear graphic style; an art that was neither bland nor abstract, but imaginative yet understandable, communicable and intelligible. Dramatic, exciting and rich in activity, it was much more than a sad remembrance of the past. So began six years of hard work, researching details, sorting through the subject matter, selecting images for the monument that had a narrative value, and constructing the clay model from which moulds would be created and castings made in the foundry.

It required the efforts of many to make the monument a reality, one of whom was London-born Irishman Edward McManus, monument co-ordinator and a member of the fundraising committee. His responsibilities saw him organise and deliver objects of historical value to Paul Day's workshop in rural France so that there would be no flaws in the authenticity of the monument's presentation. Demanding as this was, more onerous by far was the drawing up of a definitive list of the Battle of Britain participants; further difficulties came from the fact that not all the aircrew were British – they were from throughout the Commonwealth, occupied Europe and even neutral countries, including New Zealand, Australia, Canada, South Africa, Southern Rhodesia (now Zimbabwe), Belgium, France, Poland, Czechoslovakia, the United States and Ireland. RAF records were incomplete, destroyed in bombing raids. There were omissions and errors and, even if records were available, sometimes confusion arose because of the use of nicknames – well known and identifiable at the time, but this was not necessarily the case six decades later. Also, the spelling of overseas participants' names, particularly those from Poland and Czechoslovakia, threw up its own challenges. Nonetheless, their earnest involvement demanded that everything was done with precision, and with much dedication and thoroughness, a final register of names was finally reached.

It was an undoubtedly special and worthy pursuit but, nonetheless, financial resources were necessary to fund the project and the Right Honourable Lord Tebbit acted as Chairman of the Fundraising Committee. Appeals and functions were organised in the effort to realise the £1.65 million target. In the event, a disappointing response was elicited from corporate and governmental indifference and apathy. Nor was any portion of it secured from Heritage Lottery Funding. In the end, once the situation became known through the media, the cause was backed by an outraged benefactor and ordinary individuals whose small but numerous contributions made up the necessary amount. The monument recreated the drama of the battle so a new generation could see meaning in the actions of those who maintained their freedoms – actions that otherwise might be taken for granted. The monument was unveiled on 18 September 2005 by HRH The Prince of Wales.

An Irish documentary film, *Spitfire Paddy: The Ace with the Shamrock*, was directed by Gerry Johnston and made over four years. The film was released in 2017 and tells the story of 'Paddy' Finucane, famous in Britain but little-known in Ireland, regarded as one of the RAF's top fighter pilots during the Second World War and the Battle of Britain; at 21 years of age he was the youngest ever wing commander to hold the rank. He downed thirty-two enemy aircraft in just two years. His reputation, secured in interviews conducted by the BBC, made him a celebrity; in fact, he was one part of a then-celebrity couple – his girlfriend, Jean Wilford, known as 'the girl (second) next door'. His life, however, was tragically short-lived; he was killed in action, when just 21 years of age, on 15 July 1942. So ended the thrilling but tragic tale of the Dubliner who became a wartime fighter ace, a hero and a legend.

The aftermath of the Battle of Britain saw the war's theatre of operations swing east with Hitler's invasion of Russia – the opening of the Eastern Front. Failing to gain air superiority during the Battle of Britain and invade southern England and Ireland, Hitler had left the back door open for the Allies to ultimately prise open the Western Front with an invasion of their own on D-Day, 6 June 1944. This was the window of opportunity by which freedom and democracy were defended. The western world was made safe by the will and sacrifice of its soldiers, politicians and people – Irish men and women prominent among them, many in fact taking pride of place among the active participants of those who brought freedom about.

CHRONOLOGY OF THE BATTLE OF BRITAIN

1940	Event
10 May	Germany invades the Low Countries and France.
31 May	Draft plans for invasion of England presented to Hitler.
June	Evacuation of British Expeditionary Force from Dunkirk.
25 June	Fall of France.
03 July	German Air Force (Luftwaffe) begin repeated attacks on Channel shipping and ports.
10 July	Battle of Britain official start date.
16 July	Hitler issues his 'Directive 16' for Operation Sea Lion (Seelöwe), the invasion of southern England.
19 July	Hitler offers his 'final peace ultimatum' in speech in the Reichstag (German Parliament).
08 August	Luftwaffe decides to switch targets to Fighter Command's airfields.

12 August	German shelling commences on Dover and southern shoreline from long-range coastal battery in Pas de Calais. The guns were finally overrun on 26 September 1944.
13 August	Adlertag (Eagle Day). The all-out offensive from the Luftwaffe, who lose forty-five aircraft.
15 August	Black Thursday witnesses heaviest fighting in the battle to date. The Luftwaffe loses seventy-five aircraft.
18 August	The Hardest Day. Huge Luftwaffe attacks on 11 Group's airfields in search of an all-out victory; succeeds in causing considerable damage but serious losses are suffered in doing so.
24 August	Bombs mistakenly fall on central London.
25 August	The RAF bomb Berlin.
31 August	Heavy Luftwaffe raids on airfields continue.
05 September	Deliberate decision for bombing raids to begin on London as the Luftwaffe shifts its target to the capital.
07 September	Largest Luftwaffe bomber force yet assembled hits London's docks and bombing intensifies over the following days.
15 September	The Greatest Day. The day decreed that the Luftwaffe was to shatter Fighter Command, only they do not succeed in doing so.
17 September	Hitler postpones Operation Sea Lion indefinitely.
30 September	Luftwaffe bomber losses seriously mounting, day-time raids begin to be carried out by fighter bombers instead. Bomber night-time raids continue.

| 29 October | Italian aircraft commence raids on southern England. |
| 31 October | Official end to Battle of Britain. 544 RAF pilots had been killed. |

Appendix 2

LIST OF ACCREDITED BATTLE OF BRITAIN SQUADRONS

The following is a list of accredited Battle of Britain squadrons and other units which officially took part in the Battle of Britain:

1, 1 (RCAF), 3, 17, 19, 23, 25, 29, 32, 41, 43, 46, 54, 56, 64, 65, 66, 72, 73, 74, 79, 85, 87, 92, 111, 141, 145, 151, 152, 213, 219, 222, 229, 232, 234, 235, 236, 238, 242, 245, 247, 248, 249, 253, 257, 263, 264, 266, 302, 303, 310, 312, 501, 504, 600, 601, 602, 603, 604, 605, 607, 609, 610, 611, 615, 616, 804 (FAR), 808 (FAA). Plus 421 Flight, 422 Flight and the Fighter Interception Unit.

Appendix 3

LOCATION OF RAF FIGHTER COMMAND, 31 JULY 1940

No 10 Group

Airfields	Squadrons
Middle Wallop	238 Hurricane
	609 Spitfire
Filton	8 AACU Various
Exeter	213 Hurricane
	87 Hurricane
Pembrey	92 Spitfire
St Eval (Coastal	234 Spitfire
Command Station)	
Aston Down	50TU Spitfire and Blenheims
Sutton Bridge	60TU Hurricane
Hawarden	70YU Hurricane and Spitfire

No 11 Group

Airfields	Squadrons
Northolt	1 Hurricane
Kenley	64 Spitfire
	615 Spitfire

Airfields	Squadrons
Hawkinge	79 Hurricane
Biggin Hill	32 Hurricane
	610 Spitfire
Gravesend	604 Blenheim
North Weald	56 Hurricane
	151 Hurricane
Hornchurch	54 Spitfire
	65 Spitfire
Tangmere	43 Hurricane
	145 Hurricane
	601 Hurricane
	F10 Blenheim
Southend	74 Spitfire
Manston	600 Blenheim
Croydon	1 (Canadian) Hurricane
	501 Hurricane
	111 Hurricane
Hendon	257 Hurricane
	24 Various

No 12 Group

Airfields	Squadrons
Debden	85 Hurricane
	17 Hurricane
Martlesham	25 Blenheim
Duxford	19 Spitfire
	264 Defiant
Wittering	266 Spitfire
	23 Blenheim
	229 Hurricane

Airfields	Squadrons
Digby	611 Spitfire
	46 Hurricane
	29 Blenheim
Kirton in Lindsey	222 Spitfire
	253 Hurricane
Coltshall	66 Spitfire
	242 Hurricane

No 13 Group

Airfields	Squadrons
Catterick	41 Spitfire
	219 Blenheim
Church Fenton	73 Hurricane
Leconfield	616 Spitfire
	249 Hurricane
Usworth	607 Hurricane
Turnhouse	141 Defiant
	245 Hurricane
Drem	602 Spitfire
	605 Hurricane
Grangemouth (22 Group Station)	263 Hurricane
Wick (Coastal Command Station)	3 Hurricane
Castletown	504 Hurricane
Dyce (Coastal Command Station)	603 (1 flight) Spitfire
Montrose (Flying Training Command Station)	603 (1 flight) Spitfire
Acklington	152 Spitfire
	72 Spitfire

Appendix 4
R/T CODES

Code Word	Meaning
ANGELS	Height in thousands of feet
BANDIT	Enemy aircraft
BOGEY	Unidentified aircraft
BUSTER	Maximum cruising speed
GATE	Maximum speed (limited to five minutes)
LINER	Economical cruising speed
ORBIT	Circle giving point or present position
PANCAKE	Land, refuel and re-arm
SAUNTER	Minimum cruising speed
SCRAMBLE	Take-off
TALLYHO	About to attack
VECTOR	Course to steer

BIBLIOGRAPHY

Eriksson, Patrick, *Alarmstart: The German Fighter Pilots' Experience in the Second World War* (Gloucestershire: Amberley Publishing, 2017).

Holmes, Tony, *Spitfire v Bf 109 Battle of Britain* (Oxford: Osprey Publishing, 2007).

McElhinney, Paul, *The Lion of the RAF: The Extraordinary Life of George Beamish, Second World War Hero and Rugby Star* (Amberley Books, 2019).

Military Gallery, *Their Finest Hour: The Battle of Britain, 1940* (Buckinghamshire: Griffin International Limited, 2015).

Overy, Richard, *The Battle of Britain: Myth and Reality* (London: Penguin Books, 2010).

Price, Alfred, *Spitfire: Pilots' Stories* (Gloucestershire: The History Press, 2018).

Saunders, Andy, *Battle of Britain: RAF Operations Manual* (Somerset: Haynes Publishing, 2015).

Stokes, Doug, *Paddy Finucane: Fighter Ace* (Manchester: Crécy Publishing Limited, 2015).

Stokes, Doug, *Wings Aflame* (London: William Kimber & Co. Limited, 1985).

Townshend Bickers, Richard, *The Battle of Britain: The Greatest Battle in the History of Air Warfare* (London: Salamander Books Ltd, 1990).

Vigors, Tim, *Life's Too Short to Cry* (London: Grub Street, 2008).

GLOSSARY

Ack Ack	Anti-aircraft fire or 'flak'
BMG	British modified grid
C-in-C	Commander-in-chief
CO	Commanding officer
CRO	Civilian repair organisation
FAA	Fleet Air Arm
F/O	Flight officer
GSM	General situation map
HQ	Headquarters
NCO	Non-commissioned officer
OTU	Operational training unit
PO	Pilot officer
POW	Prisoner of war
RAF	Royal Air Force
RDF	Radio direction finding or 'Radar' (radio direction and ranging)
Readiness States	'Released' – Not required
	'Available' – Fifteen minutes (availability to take-off)
	'Readiness' – Five minutes (availability to take-off)

	'Stand-By' – Pilots in cockpits with engines running
RT	Radio telephone
WAAF	Women's Auxiliary Air Force
WT	Wireless telephone
UT	Under training
Vics	V-shaped formation

INDEX

Index

Index

Hitler, Adolf, 5–6, 7, 62, 83, 86–7, 92, 93, 97; and bellicosity and posturing, 23, 32; and hopes for a British surrender and armistice, 9, 13; and preparations for an invasion, 33, 39; and tactical decisions, 72, 85

Hurley, Jerry, 74

Ievers, Norman Lancelot, 80–1

Igoe, Sqn Ldr Bill, 37–8

injuries and disfigurements, 91

intercepts, 2, 23, 25, 36, 43, 45, 46, 48, 63, 65–6, 71, 80, 83, 84

internment of German prisoners in Ireland, 19–20, 21

IRA, the, 15

Irish Aer Corps, the, 93–4

Irish Defence Forces' strategy, 15–16, 17, 18–19, 21

Irish government defence spending, 17

Irish nurses in wartime Britain, 49–50

Irish Press, The (newspaper), 90–1

Irish Times, The (newspaper), 55

'Jabo' (modified fighter-bombers), 77

Johnston, Gerry, 96

Kee, Sgt Ernest Henry Clarke, 81

Kilmartin, John Ignatius, 57–8

Kyck, Kurt, 20

Leigh-Mallory, Air Vice Marshal Trafford, 33, 70

Life's Too Short to Cry (book), 93

losses, xv, 1, 36, 39, 42, 44, 46, 49, 60–1, 85, 92–3, 96; of Luftwaffe, 41, 45, 52, 69, 76–7, 84; of RAF, 39, 40, 55, 56–7, 59, 65, 69, 71–2, 77, 82

Lovell, Anthony Desmond Joseph, 68–9

Lovell, Flight Lt S.J., 69

Luftwaffe, the, vii, viii, xv, 28–30, 41, 44, 54, 59, 60–1, 62, 82, 83–4; and bomber escort role of fighter pilots, 45–6, 85; and focus on London, 63, 65–6, 68, 76; initial confidence of, 9, 32–3, 84; losses and impact on morale, 69, 76

Lynch, Fr Charlie, 92–3

Lynch, Jack, 4

Mackenzie, Kenneth William, 78–9

Maguire, Harold John, 88–90

McAdam, John, 65

McCann, Thomas Andrew, 82

McConnell, William Winder, 34–5

McCormack, John Bernard, 51–2

McManus, Edward, xii, 22, 95

McNeill, Maj Gen Hugo, 17

McSweeney, Eileen (Eil), 50, 51

medals and honours, 35, 36, 52, 56, 57, 58, 64, 67, 68, 71, 73, 79, 81, 90

memoirs, 11, 93

Memoirs of Field-Marshal the Viscount Montgomery of Alamein, The (book), 11

merchant shipping convoy attacks, 32, 33, 39, 40, 42

military significance of the Battle of Britain, 86, 92, 97

mock dogfights, 29

modifications, 77, 85–6

Molders, Maj Werner, 65, 68

Montgomery, Cecil Robert, 49

Montgomery, Gen Bernard Law, 11–12

Moore, Cecilia, xi, xii

Moore, Flight Off William, xi–xii

Moore, William Storey, 36

morale and confidence, 71, 84, 85; of the Luftwaffe, 9, 32–3

Morris, Mary, 49–50

Morris, Michael, 50

Morrogh-Ryan, Oliver Bertram, 64–5

Munich Agreement, the, 23

munitions production, 22, 87

Narrow Margin, The (book), 93

nationalities of RAF pilots, 34–5, 95

Nesham, CPl Robertina ('Robina'), 58–9

neutrality policy, 14, 18

night fighting, 36, 40

North-Bomford, Capt David John, 90–1

Observer Corps, the, 26, 41, 45, 84, 87

O'Byrne, Sgt Peter, 71–2

O'Byrne, Sgt Thomas Patrick, 72

Oflag VI-B POW camp, 79

Operation Eagle Attack (Unternehmen Adlerangriff), 47

Operation Market Garden, 12

Operation Sea Lion, 8, 72, 82, 84

Operation Viking Raid, 17–18

OTUs (Operational Training Units), 34, 35, 43, 58, 88

III

Index